Serving
LOCAL
SCHOOLS

ALSO BY CHUCK BOMAR

College Ministry 101
College Ministry from Scratch
Worlds Apart: Understanding the Mindset
and Values of 18–25 Year Olds

Serving
LOCAL
SCHOOLS

{ BRING CHRIST'S *compassion* TO
THE CORE OF YOUR *community* }

CHUCK BOMAR

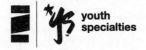

ZONDERVAN

Serving Local Schools
Copyright © 2017 by Chuck Bomar

This title is also available as a Zondervan ebook.

Requests for information should be addressed to:
Zondervan, *3900 Sparks Dr. SE, Grand Rapids, Michigan 49546*

ISBN 978–0–310–67107–7

Cover design: Brand Navigation
Cover photography: © Guillermo del Olmo Pintado/123RF
Interior design: Kait Lamphere

16 17 18 19 20 21 22 23 24 /DHV/ 15 14 13 12 11 10 9 8 7 6 5 4 3 2 1

Sayla, this book is dedicated to you.
My hope is that the contents of this book will
somehow contribute to you experiencing
the beauty of the Christian community
serving those in need, at your school.
Karis, Hope, and Sayla, my girls . . .
I love you so much!

CONTENTS

ACKNOWLEDGMENTS

There are a few people I need to mention because in my mind, they are major contributors to this book.

First, my wife, Barbara. The time and energy you put into developing relationships through serving at local schools is a constant encouragement to me. I am honored to serve alongside you!

Second, my assistant, Ellie Hughes. Thank you for your hard work researching, editing, and contributing your thoughts. I am so thankful for your genuine love for the people in our city.

Third, the Tigard/Tualatin School District employees. There are *far too many* people worthy of noting to assure I mention everyone here. So, it may be seen as a cop-out, but I am honestly too fearful of missing someone.

Fourth, Daniel Delgado. The bottom line is you helped me with this book at a point when I needed it most. This book would not have ever been written without your gifts of organization and planning. I am so grateful.

Start Here

If you want to experience the joys of the Christian life on an average day, I really think this book will be of use to you. Many people know enough about the Bible to feel guilty but haven't gone far enough with Jesus in everyday life to experience the joy of following him. I want to help with this.

This book is designed to bring awareness to an enormous opportunity and provide practical ways to express your faith. I have designed this book to inspire and equip you and your church with a vision and strategy for reaching into the core of your community through serving in your local public schools.

If your church wants to discover the real needs of your community and have a lasting impact through meeting those needs, start with the closest public school.

If you want to follow the example of Jesus and extend God's love to the disadvantaged, start with the public school.

If you want to build relationships with people across

the socioeconomic spectrum in your zip code, start with the local public school.

If you want to teach your children how to notice the needs of others where they live, start by getting involved at a local public school.

I live in Portland, Oregon, which is one of the most liberal cities in the United States, and I have found one thing to be true: schools want us involved. If this is true for me, it is at least possible for you. Your local public school is an extremely strategic place for you and your church to build relationships and serve; to be afforded opportunities to meet needs that otherwise go overlooked.

That said, this book doesn't contain a secret formula. No magic wand included. The principles in this book are simple and actionable, and the stories show how simple things can be. The chapters are filled with practical ideas and stories of people like you who are engaging in what God is doing in and through local schools. They are finding meaning through serving people in their community. There is no claim in this book that the school district is *the* way or that it is superior to other forms of community service. However, I do believe it is one of the best ways, and after reading this book I think you will agree.

I'm convinced that serving local schools is an underutilized opportunity. Not enough churches are intentionally serving the schools in their community. A lot of things contribute to the lack of participation. Churches are afraid of blurring the lines between church and state. Many live in fear because they don't understand the extent to which community members can be involved at local schools.

Thankfully, more and more people are catching on.

And it is fun.

There are how-to's and warnings in the following pages.

I will talk about why we do some things and why we should avoid pursuing other things.

I will tell stories of what people have done and hope they inspire you to write your own.

The first part of this book will help you see why I promote working with schools as one of the most effective ways of living out our faith where we live. This book is rooted in the story of my life and my process of leading our church into the core of our community. It is unique and has impacted my perspective on ministry in public schools in huge ways.

This book is *not* about which method of schooling is the best for Christians. You might have your children home schooled or in a private school. I have no interest in your educational choices for your children. I'm not advocating for any one way parents should educate their children. I am asserting that the public education sector is one of the most important means for being in touch with the core of your community.

I believe it is critical for every church to engage local public schools on some level.

If you want to know your community beyond your immediate circle of friends, get involved with the public schools.

I know many people start books and don't finish them. If you make it past chapter 1 and read at least the remainder of the first section (chapters 2 and 3), you will discover the biblical and foundational reasons behind my passion on this topic. The truths I discuss in those chapters have proven to be challenging for me, my church, and my friends.

Jesus makes me uncomfortable. Every time I read the Bible, I feel confronted by the nature of God and the life of Jesus. The first part of this book starts off the conversation by focusing on what the Bible tells us about God. It is both beautiful and convicting. And, this is where the first section of the book will end. It is a foundational section that sets the premise of the following section, which is hyperpractical.

The second section will begin in chapter 4 by telling the stories of everyday people. You will read real-life stories of people who are part of our church as well as others who are not. They are busy like everyone else. They are trying to balance life with kids, and most are engaging in successful careers. They all have one thing in common: they are serving in some way with an individual school or the school district. My hope is that you will be encouraged by their stories and personally step further into the core of the community in which you live.

After this chapter, we will move on to learn about some creative and strategic ways people have built long-term trust with schools (chapters 5 and 6). These chapters provide direction and ideas for taking steps in the right direction—for you personally or your church. I explain key positions to connect with at both the district and local school levels. I will consider these chapters successful if they simply help you walk away with a couple of ideas that get your mind going so that you can take some steps toward engaging more deeply in your community.

Chapter 7 discusses the common questions and fears around the issue of serving in local schools. There is much talk about separation of church and state and what the law says. Most people don't really understand these issues, and this causes all sorts of problems. We'll look at some of those issues in this chapter. I have found that our lack of understanding too often allows fear to direct our actions. I don't see this as being helpful for anyone, which is why I wanted to dedicate an entire chapter to this topic. You will gain clarity on the background to our current laws, and it will help in navigating the lines they draw for us. None of those lines should be crossed, but we can walk those lines with wisdom and faithfulness, and I think I can help you do just that.

Chapter 8 will likely provide some surprising information about cultural shifts that will hopefully impact how you think about where you live. I talk about three different contexts of society. One of them will be the one you live in, but you will have the opportunity to see how the other two contexts differ from yours. The other contexts can really help us see our own in a new light. And that is my hope for this chapter. I will wrap up by describing some very practical nonthreatening ways you can join in with what God is doing in your local school.

Finally, the appendices expand on the Safe Families program and Compassion Clinics that I mention throughout the book. Hopefully they will be helpful tools for you if you want to implement something similar where you live.

All that said, the goal of this book is simple: to help the average Christian fruitfully engage their community. I believe the local public schools provide the means for this like no other.

So, if you turn the page, I will start by sharing a conversation that opened up a whole new world where I began to see just how powerful working with the public school system really is . . .

The Why

CHAPTER 1

WHY PUBLIC SCHOOLS?

As I read the email on my screen I felt like I was back in elementary school being called into the principal's office. I could feel the nervous pit in my stomach.

The email was from the HR director of our school district, asking to meet with me.

Because I am a pastor, whenever I'm asked to meet with a public official, I immediately think about that line separating church and state. I tried not to assume anything negative, but I couldn't help wonder—*had I done something wrong?* I was certain that I must have crossed a line somewhere or said or done something to cross that boundary. Why else would he be asking me to come in for a meeting?

I recall feeling that same pit in my stomach as a kid when waiting to be disciplined by my mom. Waiting to be punished is a horrible experience. My waiting was compounded by the fact that the principal would call my mother and explain things, so my mom always knew all about the dumb things I had done that day at school. I would have to sit through my classes during the day, waiting to head home and take whatever she wanted to dish out.

The worst times were when I would get in trouble in the morning. The waiting would last all day. I remember when I was in sixth grade and I wore shorts to school. My mom never allowed this, so I would put the shorts on underneath my pants. On my way to school I would then stop somewhere, take the pants off, and stuff them in my backpack. I did this day after day until one day I not only changed into my shorts after I left the house, but I also decided to take the city bus instead of the school bus.

As I approached the city bus stop that morning (with my shorts on), my mom pulled up in her car beside me. She rolled down the passenger window, looked at me standing there in my shorts (at the wrong bus stop), and uttered one sentence: "I will deal with you when I get home from work." That was all she said. Then she rolled up the window and drove away.

It was a long day.

I was filled with horrible anticipation, and for most of the day, my face was fire hydrant red and the lump in my throat felt like a watermelon. This memory conveys a bit how I felt after I finished reading the email from the school's HR director. But this time I didn't know what I had done wrong.

Though I had one guess. It might have something to do with my request.

Let me back up a bit. I had moved to Portland, Oregon eighteen months earlier to reach and serve the city by planting a church. It is my conviction that churches should be a resource to serve the community. We wanted to help the people around us, so we decided to host a free medical and dental clinic. As we looked around for a good location to host the clinic, we settled on our local public school. The school had rooms and facilities that could be rented out, so we turned in a request to the school district to ask if we could use the local high school for the clinic. Our initial request was almost immediately denied. We were told the school was booked on the day we wanted. So we sent in a second request for a different date, and that was denied as well. This time the letter of denial came with a very clear response: *We apologize but the high school is booked out for the entire 2009–2010 school year.*

I wasn't sure how to receive this. I had a difficult time believing that the school was completely booked up *every* Saturday for the *entire* school year. Because all requests for building use have to go through our district office, they could have easily suggested another school campus for us to utilize. But that was not the case here. So we were left wondering, what was the real problem?

I let everyone at our church who was interested in helping with the clinic know about the situation. I simply told them to pray and wait. We needed God to do something. We weren't coming with a hidden agenda. We were Christians offering ourselves as a resource to serve our community, and this clinic was a genuine reflection of our faith. So we prayed and we asked God to open doors for us to extend his love to those in need living among us.

That was two weeks before the email from the HR director showed up in my inbox. So even though I still had that anxious pit in my stomach, part of me was also looking forward to having a conversation with our school leaders. Before I had moved to Portland, I had spent time praying from my living room in Southern California, asking that God would give me favor with the school district. I had specifically asked God to give our church a "unique relationship" with them. Could this be the answer to those prayers? Was God doing something here? I hoped so, but I wasn't sure. It could also be a way of formally shutting the door. I couldn't tell, so I accepted the invitation and plugged it into my calendar.

THE HEARTBEAT OF EVERY CONTEXT

Life in every community revolves around a different center. College towns revolve around the university calendar. Local restaurants are busy from September through April, and then the rhythm changes during the summer months. Life in the urban core of large cities like New York City, where many don't own cars, revolves around the traditional idea of neighborhood—the local coffee shop, the dry cleaner, and the grocery store. In suburban contexts, where hardly anything is centralized, activities for kids tend to determine the life cycle. Minivans and SUVs fill the parking lots around sports fields and shopping malls. In more rural areas, everyday life is driven by agricultural cycles. There is a harvest time where everyone is working from sunup to sundown. Winter comes, the time when repairs to fences are made and chores inside the home or barns are taken care of.

Life has different cycles that vary from context to context, from place to place.

Yet in almost every community there is one place where you can sense the heartbeat of the people who live there. You won't find everyone hanging out at the dry cleaner or even at the coffee shop in the urban core. In the suburbs, you'll see people taking their kids to sports activities, but not every child will excel at athletics. But every type of person—a broad and diverse cross-section of the community—will be connected in some way to the public schools. If you want to know the pulse of your community, get to know your local public school. Get to know the teachers and the administrators. They are on the front lines, dealing with the socioeconomic diversity of the area.

We tend to live around people who have a similar socioeconomic status. Sure, there is usually some variance between our friends, but in general people tend to live closest to others like them. People of privilege easily drive past a disadvantaged neighborhood without giving it a second thought. And those living in rundown apartments rarely make it to the neighborhoods of the affluent. We all live in our separate worlds, and rarely do those worlds meet or collide.

But that's exactly what you'll find in most public schools. There is a world of diversity right within their walls because the schools draw from multiple neighborhoods. In the schools, the socioeconomic variance we see as we drive past the neighborhoods in our community is not just seen—it is felt and experienced. Tensions inevitably surface and have to be dealt with by those working within the schools. Public schools carry an enormous weight of expectation and responsibility today—far more than they can bear. They experience every conceivable social issue that is present in a community, including homelessness, racial diversity, family instability, and mental health.

I realize that I'm speaking in broad generalities. Some might suggest that there are other avenues in a community to experience and address these issues. And I'll agree that there is some truth in this objection. Each community is different, and some communities may find that a local rec center or some other organization brings the community together in a unique way. But if you look across our country and even many places around the world today, there are few places that truly rival the local public school in bringing together diverse people from all parts of a community. There is no other system that draws families and children in the same way.

This is why I chose to focus my prayers by asking that God would grant our church a unique relationship with the school district. As I was praying from my living room in Southern California, I only had a vague sense of what was possible. At that time, I could not articulate what I now have come to believe. But it was still evident to me that the best way to serve my community was to serve the school. I knew with conviction that the heartbeat of a community is found by engaging the local public school.

So I was both nervous and excited at the invitation to meet with the HR director. Excited because I wondered if this might be the answer to our prayers. Nervous because I was afraid that the school might be throwing up some roadblocks and barriers to prevent us from getting to know them better. It felt like I had come to a fork in the road, as if this one conversation would set a trajectory for our church in two possible directions. It could be an onramp to further service and relationship with our school or a wall that would stop us in our tracks. I wasn't sure what to expect. The email didn't give me any hints.

And my concerns went well beyond the relationship between our church and the school. I am a pastor, but I also have children who are educated in this school system. My kids attend the public school, and while I wanted those working within the school system to know that I was a Christian, I didn't want them to make negative assumptions about me and attach them to my children because I'm a pastor. I wanted them to know me as a parent who cares about the needs of the city. I wanted them to know that I am a Christian who wants to serve and help people in need. I didn't have a lot of money to offer, but I could follow Jesus' example by offering myself wherever I was most needed.

THE MEETING

The day of the meeting finally arrived. We sat down, briefly went around the table to introduce ourselves, and I explained to the HR director why I was there: I believe Jesus is who he says he is, and he was why I wanted to help the school.

Maybe you're wondering—was that really the best approach? Some people are surprised to hear that I was so direct and honest in sharing all this. After all, if there is one person you *wouldn't* want to say all these things to, it's probably the HR director of your local school district.

But I had a good reason for doing that. Let me explain.

What I haven't mentioned yet is that I called a friend before I went to the meeting. I phoned my friend Kevin Palau and asked him if he would join me for the meeting. If you don't know who Kevin is, he is the son of evangelist Luis Palau and the president of the Luis Palau Association, which has its headquarters in the Portland metro area. The Luis Palau organization is known for their evangelistic work around the world. But what many people don't realize is that in addition to their global work, the organization has had a tremendous influence in the local Portland area as well. Kevin has led the charge on this and has worked very hard to come alongside civic leaders in the city, partnering with them on a number of projects. Since I was the "new guy" in the city, I thought it would be wise to reach out to someone who had a reputation and a proven track record. So I called Kevin and asked him to join me. Kevin didn't know the HR director at the time, but we learned that the director was aware of the Palau organization's involvement in a number of citywide initiatives. I hoped that having Kevin with me would help set the tone for our conversation and give us a place to begin building a relationship.

When we arrived at the district offices, we signed in at the front desk and waited for someone to bring us to the meeting. I had believed that Kevin and I were meeting alone with the HR director, but it turned out I was wrong. We were taken to a room with a massive conference table and met the HR director and two other district employees. It was a little awkward at first, but after the HR director introduced everyone, he then turned the conversation over to the woman on his left.

She began by asking me a very direct question: "Chuck, why do you want to do this clinic? I have been told that it's because of your faith; can you explain that?"

To be honest, I wasn't expecting to jump into this right away. I was thinking we would have some small talk and get to know each other a bit. But that wasn't going to happen. So I jumped right in. I didn't know this woman, and I didn't know why she was asking me. Was she a Christian, hoping that I would voice her own Christian faith to the others in the room? Or was she opposed to all of this and trying to clearly draw a line in the sand to block our intentions? I looked around the table for some guidance in how to proceed, but all three of the district employees were wearing perfect poker faces.

I decided to give it my best shot and answer her question. I explained why I wanted to help, and I took a few minutes to share who I believe Jesus is. I talked about his selfless life as the imprint of God's love for the world. I shared that I see helping others in need as a genuine expression of my faith. I told them that I believed that *not* offering myself in this way would be hypocritical and wrong. I also let them know that I understood that they might have concerns partnering with a church and with me as a pastor. But I asked them to give me a chance to earn their trust, to prove that we wanted to help and serve. I also mentioned that I knew that they might have a fear that I would voice my faith in the schools. I told them that I understood those fears and I would be careful with expressing my faith; however I could never apologize for why I wanted to help others. Jesus was the reason, period.

For the most part, my friend Kevin sat there quietly. He shared a bit about how he viewed the church as a resource and how this was occurring more in our city. There was an awkward silence after I finished talking. The HR director asked some specific questions about the clinic itself. I answered honestly, letting them know that I wanted to work in partnership with them because they knew the needs of our community far better than I did. At that, they broke from their poker faces. It was obvious that they at least agreed with that statement.

When the meeting was over, Kevin and I walked out. We had no idea what the outcome would be. I had tried to explain my faith tactfully, but I had also been pretty blunt about who I was and what I believed. There was part of me that wondered if my honesty had backfired—if this was the beginning of the end of my relationship with the school district.

I had shared the gospel. I had told these public school officials that Jesus was the reason why I was there. Certainly, we had also talked over the practical benefits of the clinic. We all knew that there were people in our community who lacked medical and dental insurance. They would greatly benefit from the care we could provide. And we all knew that budgets had decreased over the past few years. We all understood that there was a real need for resources, both financial and volunteer help. Still, I had doubts. Had my honesty crossed that line separating the church from the state? Had I gone too far?

THE CLINIC AND OPENED DOORS

I later discovered that the HR director is not a Christian. But he was also aware of the unmet needs in the community. And he knew that his employees—the teachers and administrators in the local schools—were bearing the load of trying to teach with those needs unmet. And here was someone knocking at his door offering help and resources. Here was someone who admitted that he didn't fully know the need, who saw himself and his organization as a helpful and necessary part of the community.

You might expect me to say that our meeting led to wonderful relationships with these individuals that has developed over several years. But that's not what happened. In fact, today I could walk right by the three district employees we met with that day and not recognize them. To my knowledge we have not spoken since that meeting. But a week after our meeting, we received a formal response. The email let me know that they had reserved the high school for us to use on Saturday, October 13th. In addition, the facility was ours to use as a donation—there would be no cost. This surprised me more than anything, since renting the district facilities *always* had a cost. If nothing else, they charged you for the janitorial costs.

But for our clinic, there was no charge at all.

And that's not all. The school district helped us by sending out letters to every family on the meal plan. This is a list of families who live at or below the poverty level. Children on the list are served a free breakfast and lunch every day while at school. On top of that, the district office also sent out a total of twenty-two thousand flyers inviting people to our clinic. They used their automated phone system to notify every family in the district about what the clinic provided and then paid for commercial announcements on a Spanish radio and television station in our area out of their own budget.

I was speechless. In fact, I still get chills as I write that out.

It was such a sweet moment.

Prayers had been answered.

Over one thousand people were served that first day at our clinic. Appointments began at 8:00 a.m., but a line had already formed outside the school by 6:00 a.m. Kids, moms and dads, grandparents . . . all of them were there waiting to be served and cared for. There was so much need that, sadly, we had to turn some people away.

What became abundantly clear to me through this experience was just how connected the school district was to the people in need in our city. As a trusted public channel they had relational and practical connection points with countless individuals in need. I had assumed this was true, but until we began working at the clinic I had no idea *how* true it was. Working on the clinic exposed our church to the full reach of the public school system.

We provided free fillings and extractions for those with dental needs. We were even able to provide dentures for three adults. I still remember the look on their faces when they put them in and looked in the mirror. Priceless. People came to see doctors and received free prescriptions. Others had their vision checked and were given new glasses free of charge. Still others received immunizations or saw a chiropractor for their back or a podiatrist for their feet.

The clinic was more than a success. It was a game-changer. We have continued to host this clinic in partnership with the school district and an organization called Compassion Connect ever since that day. We've also received $10,000 each year out of the city budget to assist us with the costs associated in running these clinics. As I write, we are now doing two of them and are always looking for opportunities to do more.

Clinics are not the only thing a church can do. And they aren't even the primary focus of our service in the community. But the clinic was our first foray into working with the school, and it gave us a glimpse of how overwhelming the needs were and the opportunities we had in working with the school district. None of us really understood the potential when we started. And we certainly didn't see the extent of the need. That's partly because there were few people engaging with our school district in these ways. It was a unique time in shaping our small role as a church in the city, and it would prove to be the start of a meaningful and long-term relationship with our school district. They had been dealing with these needs for years, but they had never had help or assistance like we offered. Now, unexpectedly, they were receiving the much-needed assistance they had longed for.

Many of our volunteers were shocked when they first saw the need that existed right there in our community, in our neighborhoods, among the people living down the street and next door. But none of the school district employees who came that day seemed even slightly surprised. They knew of the need. And it was at that point I realized that our church and the others that helped us run the clinic had been disconnected from our city. We had been vaguely aware of the needs but largely oblivious to the full scale of the problem.

Because of this event, we've now come to the conviction that the public schools have the heartbeat of the city at their fingertips. They provide the perfect pathway for us to be who we are called to be and to reflect who we believe God to be. Regardless of what context you live in, as a Christian, you have a responsibility to engage people in need. And in our day and age, one of the best places to do that—perhaps *the* best—is through the public schools in your city or town.

In the pages that follow, we'll go over some of the practical ways to do all of this. But before we get there, there is a question begging to be asked: Why? Why should we as Christians engage our communities? Why should we be involved in our local schools? We need to begin by looking at the one thing that distinguishes us from everyone else who wants to help their neighbors. We'll find out what that is in the next chapter.

CHAPTER 2

SEPARATION OF CHURCH AND EVERYTHING

A friend of mine recently sat down for a meeting with the Dalai Lama.

Okay, I know what you're saying. Hold on for just a minute. How does someone get a meeting with the Dalai Lama? Is there some sort of an assistant you contact? Is there some website where you can submit a request? Or was he just lucky?

And then, there is the second question: What in the world do you talk about in a meeting like this? Would you go in with a list of questions or topics to discuss . . . or just sit and listen? What sort of expectations would you have in this situation?

I think it's safe to assume that the Dalai Lama exudes profound discernment. He must have spent a great deal of time absorbing an abnormal amount of knowledge of the Buddhist belief system to be recognized as a leader in that community. And if you are like me, you might assume that the Dalai Lama got to where he is today because he worked his way up the ladder of leadership. The Roman Catholic Church has this approach when they consider whom to appoint as the Pope. To become the leader of the global Roman Catholic community, you need to have a proven track record over many years. At the very least, it takes a lot of time to earn the respect of those voting.

However, I learned that the process of the rise of the Dalai Lama to his position was nothing like this at all. In fact, there wasn't even a process of being chosen for the position. Tibetan Buddhists believe that their leader was found, not chosen. Sounds so simple that I know it's complex. The bottom line is that he had zero choice in being where he is. He did nothing to "earn" his position. In fact, he was "found" at the ripe young age of four. In the Buddhist belief system, this position is seen as his reincarnated role for his current life. Before kindergarten age, this person was thrust into one of the most respected spiritual positions in the world today.

Let's get back to my friend. He was at this meeting because he is a Christian leader, and he was invited to the meeting with fourteen other leaders of the religious world, leaders representing every major religion.

Hindu.

Buddhist.

Jewish.

Muslim.

Again, I start to wonder . . . what would they talk about? What could possibly bring them all together? What's the universal topic that the Dalai Lama wanted to address with all of these leaders?

Peace?

Humility?

Servanthood?

How about Jesus?

. . . Jesus?

Yep. Believe it or not, Jesus was the sole topic of the discussion. The Dalai Lama wanted to talk about Jesus with a melting pot of religious leaders. He brought up the question of peace in the Middle East, and he said that Jesus was the only hope for that to happen. (Though the Dalai Lama speaks about and I'm sure models humility, pointing to Jesus as *the* role model for this way of life seemed a little crazy.) He talked about caring for the poor and again pointed to Jesus as *the* example for all to follow.

The Dalai Lama's point was crystal clear. The way of Jesus is the only way for humanity. The only hope for the world is Jesus.

I sat listening to my friend tell me about his experience as I sipped my latte. I was intrigued, as I'm sure you are as well. Why Jesus? Why would a Buddhist leader talk about him in the midst of such an odd mix of religious leaders? And how can the Dalai Lama genuinely say that Jesus is the only hope for the world, given his beliefs?

These were the questions circulating through my mind as I listened to my friend. But it was my ignorance that caused me to ask these questions.

You see, there are reasons why the Dalai Lama was the best person to host this meeting and why they talked about Jesus. The Dalai Lama knew that the leaders didn't all get along, but for whatever reason they were willing to meet with him. And he also knew that Jesus, believe it or not, is the *only person* that each of these leaders commonly esteem. Of course, most of them reject the idea that Jesus is the Son of God incarnate (in the flesh). But out of mutual respect for Jesus, they were willing to meet together and talk about him.

Jesus was unlike any man who has ever lived. He had a way about him. He was powerfully unique.

In my ignorance I assumed that those who were not Christians would have no interest in Jesus. I questioned why they would talk about him. But wisdom led the Dalai Lama to have him as the focus of the discussion. And to be abundantly clear, Jesus was the only point he made. I was surprised. I'm guessing you are too.

But should this really surprise us? Should we be surprised when we find that Jesus crosses barriers? The world holds a grudge against Christianity, against the actions of the church over history and the ways people have used Jesus for their own ends. But Jesus enjoys respect from a wide cross-section of humanity. Though many view Christianity as a Western ideology that oppresses people, Jesus is seen as a liberating teacher sent by God, someone who is a model for all humanity.

Jesus had a way about him.

My point is not to suggest that these leaders believe everything Jesus said or all he claimed to be. But I'm encouraged to hear that the Dalai Lama reads the Gospels daily to learn about and from Jesus and encourages others to do the same. And the same is true of many Muslim leaders. There are people who don't know Jesus who simply want to learn about him. They want to study his life. There is something about who Jesus was, how he lived, and ultimately how he died that intrigues people. Because of the life he lived, his teachings reach much further than many of us are aware.

His ways spoke loudly, and therefore people still listen to what he said through the life he lived.

A MATTER OF THE HEART

Jesus had a way about him.

Jesus could say things in a way that graciously silenced his detractors. He often left people musing on the depths of his most basic teachings. His articulation of reality was potent yet palatable. He was the master of the obvious. He had a way of centering life back to what is true about his Father. And when he did this, he left no room for argument.

It's no secret that the natural trajectory of human life is toward complexity. Jesus was different. He could break matters down and simplify the most complex situations. He cut straight to the heart. He didn't beat around bushes. And unlike most, he spoke truth with pointed direction and love.

The gospel of Matthew gives us a clue to how Jesus did this. In Matthew 22 we read about an encounter between Jesus and the religious elite of his day. The Pharisees had managed to take the simplicity of Scripture and create a shallow complexity baked with rules and techniques. They had fallen into the trap of equating spiritual maturity with their intellectual grasp of Scripture.

Their treatment of the Torah (the Law portion of the Old Testament) is a good example of this. For us, reading through these first five books of our Bibles can be burdensome. We grow bored with the lists of what seems to us nothing more than lifeless religious rules and regulations. However, when Jesus walked this earth, these five books were the focal point of the Jewish relationship to God. They served (and still serve) as the axis around which both Jewish life and faith revolve.

God provided his people with a simplification of the exhaustive Law in Exodus 20, a section of Scripture known as the Ten Commandments. Yet despite this summary, the Pharisees spent a great deal of time dissecting the fine points of the Law, systematizing it and creating elaborate theories. They broke it down into at least 613 different laws, articulated two major divisions of laws, and listed out 248 positive and 365 negative laws. They even developed a framework to understand the laws, naming some *heavy* laws while referring to others as *light* laws.

They had it all figured out, or so they thought.

Matthew recalls a question the religious leaders asked of Jesus. They asked Jesus what seems to be a fairly simple question.

"Teacher, which is the great commandment in the Law?"[1]

But in their minds, this wasn't a simple question to answer. It carried as much baggage as a Boeing 747. Likely, they were hoping to stump Jesus. But regardless of their motivation, they clearly assumed Jesus could not possibly narrow down their motley thoughts.

But Jesus had a way about him.

Jesus simply replied, "You shall love the Lord your God with all your heart and with all your soul and with all your mind. This is the great and first commandment."

But there was more behind Jesus' response. Much more.

Jesus knew that they had precisely articulated the 613 different laws in the Torah, but he wasn't going to engage them in a rat-wheel of debate. Instead, he cut to the heart of the matter and spoke about his Father's desire and design for humanity. He reminded them that doing the "right thing" for the wrong reason doesn't please God.

That ultimately it is not about what you do, but about who you love.

The Pharisees were trying to figure out what they needed to do most, but Jesus was reminding them that before you figure out *what* you do, you need to think about *who* you love. Who do you love most?

Just as there was more behind the question, there was more to Jesus' answer. In his response, Jesus quoted a section of Scripture known by the Jews as the Shema. The Shema could be regurgitated by Jewish men in their sleep. It was central to their everyday practices. This section of Scripture, found in Deuteronomy chapter 6, was posted on every doorpost of their homes in a small wooden box. The Shema would also be found in the pouch, known as a phylactery, worn by the Pharisees in their armpit area and on their forehead while they prayed. The Shema was always recited by the Pharisees prior to times of prayer.

This passage could not have been more familiar to those questioning Jesus.

Jesus quotes the Shema to these leaders. And some of them probably smirked and thought, that's the easy answer. But Jesus wanted them to see that they had missed something; that this passage of Scripture that they recited multiple times a day and had on every doorpost in their homes spoke of a truth that they did not live. Jesus was telling them that they had missed something really, really important. It's called the point.

Somehow in all of their highbrow "scholarly" study of the Scripture, they had missed the simple truth of the Word of God. Before anything else, we begin with our love of God. Jesus gave them a simple answer, but he also shattered the scaffolding they set up to protect themselves from ever having to change.

Jesus had a way about him.

The religious leaders were worried about what people thought. They were motivated by a concern for themselves, for their position and status, and they relished the reward of applause and approval from others. Jesus called them out. He pointed out that who they loved was what mattered most of all.

And just in case they were ready to point out that their love for God was evident in the ways they kept all the laws, Jesus gave them a second word. Again, he spoke about love. But this time, he connected their so-called love for God directly with the way they loved their neighbor. In one instance, he went so far as to define their neighbor as the person who loved the despised and cared for the outcast in need.

It was the direction of his love that set Jesus apart. He demonstrated his love for his Father by giving himself to others. His love for the Father was revealed in carrying out the mission his Father had given to him—loving the lost and redeeming those in slavery to sin.

We can't do what Jesus did for us, but we can carry on his mission, the mission he gave to his followers. We can take the love he has demonstrated for us and love others as we have been loved. We can serve as he served and ultimately point people to the Servant King who loves them. Jesus had a way about him. We have something to learn.

God as Love

Jesus wasn't interested in intellectual exercises. He spoke the language of the heart. The Pharisees believed that spiritual maturity equaled a precise understanding of every nuance of theology. They spent a lot of time studying Scripture, but they missed the point of their study—Jesus! Jesus challenged them and called them out, to something deeper than surface religious knowledge. Jesus boiled obedience down to a matter of the heart.

What you do matters. We all know this. But Jesus took it a step further. He told them that *why* they were doing what they were doing mattered most.

Before we condemn the Pharisees for missing the obvious, let's admit that there is more than a little Pharisee within each of us. We do the same things they do. We negate the heart issues by overemphasizing our outward behavior. We equate head knowledge with spiritual maturity. We even want to serve people in need without thinking through why we are doing it.

Jesus was perfect in his love. He was the sole human being who perfectly responded to the love of the Father and always appropriately reflected that love toward others. He was, in fact, the imprint of God's perfect love. This is what separated Jesus from everything else in the world, from everyone else who has ever lived.

We certainly cannot be perfect in our conduct. In fact, if we think we are, we'll fall prey to the same mistake the Pharisees made. We'll put our faith in ourselves and in our own abilities and think that in our wisdom, strength, and power we can change the world and fix the problems that plague our communities. But that's not love. That's spiritual pride.

The work of Jesus, in loving and serving those who were unloved, should humble us and leave us without spiritual pride. Of all people, we must recognize that nothing we have belongs to us. We are the recipients of grace, a love we did not deserve; and because we have been loved in this way, we naturally respond by loving others—especially those who don't "deserve" our love.

You see, as followers of Jesus, it should be our love that sets us apart. Other people can do good works, but they aren't doing them for the same reasons. This should be what separates the church (i.e., God's people) and everything else. This is what makes us unique where we live. So before we start getting practical about what it means to serve your local schools, let's talk about your motives for doing so.

We cannot simply talk about what we should do. We need to talk about *why*. And that begins with God and who he has always been. Our motivation is rooted in who God is and what he has done for us. We stand out as a light in this world when we live out our identity in God.

Before the world was created . . .

Who was God?

What would you say defined his being?

The typical answer is something like, "He is Creator." I agree. Genesis tells us about his work of creation. However, think a bit more deeply.

In time as we know it, before creation . . . what defined God at that point?

Take a few minutes to think about that . . . .

Seriously. Set this book down and sift through who you would say God was before he created the world. Think about it. Take some time. When you're ready, turn the page and continue reading.

I asked you to take a moment to reflect on who you think God is. One of the ways we make ourselves the center of everything is by making the conversation about us. We were created, we sinned, and we were separated from God. Our sins were forgiven through Jesus, and now through faith we can spend eternity with God.

But the good news of the gospel, the good news that lies underneath all the reasons why it is good news for us is *not* that we invite Jesus into our lives. The good news of the gospel is that it all begins with God. We are invited into his life!

And his life has always existed. Long before the world was created. The good news starts with God, not with his creation—with you and me and all the reasons why we need God.

So who was God before creation?

God was a relationship. Or rather, he existed as a community of loving relationships. And he still does. The Christian faith is unique in this, and it is founded on a basic truth often called the Trinity. It's a way of saying God is a relationship of Persons. We often make this highly impersonal by trying to describe the concept of the Trinity with illustrations about the different forms of water (frozen, liquid, and solid) or the different ways eggs can be eaten. But good Christian doctrine should lead us to think of the reality at the heart of all

Creation. When we see the letters G-O-D we should think of a community of relationships. God is not a concept we can try to dissect. Rather, he is a relationship we participate in.

You might be saying, "Whoa, I just wanted to read about serving in the local school. What's all this about? I didn't sign up for a theology class."

Stay with me for a moment because if you get this wrong, the methods and ideas we talk about later won't really make much of a difference, at least not in the big picture. And all of this connects to our reason for reaching out in compassion to serve and love others. We can't even read past the first chapter of Genesis and miss the fact that God is a relationship! In Genesis 1:26, God is speaking and says, "Let us make man in our image . . ."

The Bible tells us that God, as he exists in a relationship, is defined in Scripture as one thing: love (1 John 4:7–21). Love is a relational word and when it comes to God, we know this is a perfect love. It's nothing like the love we see on the big screen or even the broken love we experience in our families and friendships. It's a holy love. It always does the right thing for the right reasons, even at great personal cost. It stands for justice. It defends the innocent. It pursues the lost. It woos and confronts. And above all else, it overflows as a never-ending fountain of endless joy for those that encounter it. Before the world was created, God existed as he always was—as Father, Son, and Spirit. Nothing had been created at that point. God was who he is. But he was not lonely, in need of anything. The Father loved the Son, the Son loved the Father, and their love was perfect and purely communicated in the Person of the Holy Spirit. And it was always that way. They lived in perfect joy and affection. At the core of existence then, when you peel back all the layers, this is what you find: a triune God who IS love.

And it is out of the overflow of his love that he chooses to freely create. He isn't lonely or in need. He creates because it pleases him, because he wants to. And in doing this, he makes all that exists, including you and me. Creation then is an invitation to experience the loving relationship God has always been. Creating was a way in which God was sharing himself. God was a perfect, self-sustaining, and loving relationship. The Father was loving the Son and the Son was responding to that love (John 17:24). The Holy Spirit then was doing what he always does: communicating God's love. This is why Paul prays in Ephesians 3:14–21 for the Holy Spirit to strengthen us in our inner beings by helping us grasp the love of Jesus. It is also why Paul states in Romans 5:5 that the love of God has been "poured into our hearts through the Holy Spirit." The Holy Spirit is the One that communicates God as love to the world.

When we consider God in this way, we begin to understand ourselves as people created in his image. We are relational beings designed to love.

So when we talk about serving your local school, we're not necessarily talking about a program, though you may start something. We are not talking about a social justice project, though you may become an advocate for justice. We are simply talking about being an image bearer of a loving God.

It's far too easy to talk about Christianity as being about a relationship and then just talk about God as a concept. We study the Bible to dissect him, and then neglect the matters of the heart by overly focusing on our outward behaviors, habits, disciplines, and programs. This is our inner Pharisee. And don't misunderstand me. There is beauty in doing all these things, in seeking to grow in holiness, in reading the Bible, in establishing godly habits and disciplines. But the power of these things we do is found in the person to whom we direct our love. That's the secret of the heart that Jesus teaches to us. Who we love directs who we see ourselves to be.

I lay all of this here in the second chapter for you,

because I believe that serving public schools is not a programmatic thing we do, like attending church on Sunday morning or dropping a twenty in the offering plate. We are designed to live in a loving relationship with those around us. Serving public schools is a pathway of reflecting who God is. It is being who we are in Christ to the world around us.

Our Uniquely Directed Love

I think Jesus was getting to this dynamic in his conversations with the Pharisees. He knew the relationship he had always been part of with his Father and the Spirit (John 17:5), and he simply wanted us to experience it as well! In other words, Jesus wants us to experience the love relationship that has always existed as God. (If you don't believe me, spend some time reading John 17, taking special note of verses 20–24, and see what Jesus asks for in these verses.)

We may be able to *understand* God's love, at least as an intellectual concept. But it isn't the same as actually loving someone. The Father was always giving love to the Son and vice versa, because that's who he is. It wasn't something unnatural or awkward. His actions reflect his essence, and that love was so wonderful it was shared outwardly in creating.

Our love, however imperfect it may be, is to be like his. And that means that it is only love when it is outwardly shared. In fact, that's exactly what we celebrate on Christmas. We celebrate the reality that God shares himself with us. God's love is always giving of self, always generous with self.

"God so loved the world that he *gave* his only Son" (John 3:16, emphasis mine).

This is why Jesus is so interested in Matthew 22 about how our love is directed: toward God and others. This is the crux of what he was saying to the Pharisees: if they love God, it should flow outward to others, looking beyond themselves. In 2 Corinthians 5:14–15, the apostle Paul says that it is the self-giving love of Christ that serves as his motivator. And he is clear about the conclusion this leads him to: self-denial. He tells us that Jesus died: so "that those who live might no longer live for themselves but for him who for their sake died." It is the love of God as revealed through Christ that leads Paul to set himself aside and appropriately direct his love away from himself. All of this gives us a new identity as we are united with God in Christ (vv. 16–17). And it is because we are united to Jesus and know his love that we now take the message of reconciliation out to the world (vv. 18–19). It's what separates us from everything else.

The apostle Paul's point is simple: if we understand

God's love expressed through Jesus, we will participate in what he is doing. Our understanding of God's love will not just be something we know. It will define who we are, and it will always lead us to action. We will turn away from ourselves, toward God and others.

Jesus made this clear in Luke 9:23–25 and again in Mark 8:34–35 when he explains that if we want to experience who he is and we want to participate in his life, we must first decide to set ourselves aside. According to Jesus, the ramifications of daily denying ourselves are that we inevitably find true life. And it makes sense. If God has always been self-giving love, then as his image bearers we truly find what it means to be human by giving of ourselves and our love to others. We become thankful for union with God today, and we find it pure joy to participate in helping others experience that as well. We don't focus on what we might leave behind because we are so consumed by what we've been given.

Jesus invites us into his life and ways of directing our love toward God and others. This is what separates us from the world. How we reflect God as love will differ from person to person, but it is something that motivates every Christian to do what they do.

In our church I talk about this in a number of different ways, and I occasionally use a visual aid or diagram to help our people see this reality more clearly.

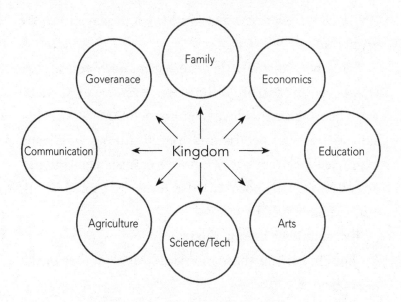

Domains of Life and Work

The image above has the kingdom of God at the center. And it points to various areas—domains of society where we live and work. The point is that the kingdom, that arena where we live under God's rule and reign, is experienced by simply seeking to reflect God as love into that area. We look to Jesus as the example for how we do this, and we rely upon his life in us (the Holy Spirit) to motivate us and empower us to do it. We seek to embed the ways of Jesus into everything we do, wherever we are. Whether we do this as a stay-at-home mom, as an educator, or an artist, our life is about expressing God's kingdom ways to those around us.

This will look a little different for each person, but this is the big picture of how the love of Christ motivates us to share that love in our own unique ways. That said, there is a specific and highly unique way Jesus expressed love that every follower of Jesus needs to pay attention to. This peculiarity of Jesus is honored by all, but it is embraced by few.

We should be among the few.

But I'm getting ahead of myself. More on that in the next chapter.

CHAPTER 3

LOVING THE MARGINALIZED

Everyone has heroes.

I'm not talking about fictional characters like Superman or Wonder Woman. I'm talking about human beings who encourage us to better ourselves—to be better people. I'm talking about the people who inspire us to move forward, who help us leave the past where it belongs and push us to plow the fields ahead. I'm referring to people who change the way we live our lives simply through the way they choose to live theirs.

Mother Teresa or Nelson Mandela or Martin Luther King, Jr. would all fall under this category of heroes. These heroes of humanity stand out from among the rest of us. They make being human attractive again. They motivate us to invest ourselves in meaningful pursuits.

But . . .

There are also heroes who live a bit closer to home. They may not be known around the world. They are never on television. No one is putting their names in a history book. You know some of them personally. They are the people who have championed over cancer, endured the loss of a child, or prevailed despite misfortune, yet always seem to be helping others. They challenge us in a way that Mother Teresa or Dr. King may not. We see their inner strength and we know their insecurities. We see them striving forward, but we also see them in times of weakness and failure. Heroes like this are a great encouragement.

We honor our heroes. But what do we honor them for? People can earn respect for doing all sorts of different things, but when you stop and think about it, those who extend dignity to marginalized people seem to be respected by everyone.

It's one of the reasons why Jesus appeals to so many.

Showing dignity to those in need is not limited to any one type of person, but Jesus chose to focus on a specific group—the poor. You can turn your Bible upside down, but you'll still find that preaching, healing, and living among the poor was central to his ministry.

And it was true for his followers as well, the early Christians. Today, everyone honors Jesus' focus on the poor, but few of us translate it into action.

THE UNIQUE HEART OF GOD

I want to suggest that Christians should focus their lives on caring for the poor and disadvantaged. Not because it's what society wants us to do, or because it's the latest trend in the church, but because it is what Jesus wants us to do. The problem is that when we think of the poor we tend to limit our thinking to the financially challenged. But the Scriptures don't limit who is "poor" in the eyes of God. The Bible describes poverty as more than a socioeconomic status. It's used in this broader way in chapter 5 of Matthew's gospel. Here Jesus makes a number of statements about who is "blessed," and in one of these statements he refers to the "poor in spirit." This refers to those who have nothing to offer others in a given moment. That can be true of those living in material poverty, to be sure, but it can also describe the suburban mom, the father who has given his life to his work, really anyone who has reached the point of emptiness or feels spiritually dead. Jesus is saying something radical here—that those who are truly blessed and happy in his kingdom are those who know they have nothing to offer others around them. God is with and for those who know they have nothing to offer anyone. They are the rejects, the ones whom the privileged of society consider failures or at the very least look past. After all, there is nothing to gain from being in relationship with them.

The poor, Jesus tells us, are blessed.

Blessing in the Scriptures doesn't refer to the absence of pain or the presence of comfort. God is with us through all of those things. It refers to the pleasure of

God and the joy that accompanies it. So Jesus is making a stark point in Matthew 5: God stands with and for the disadvantaged. God has always fought for the poor and oppressed. He has always championed those who find themselves on the outskirts of society.

And God also stands ready to confront those who stand against the poor. God confronts those who aren't willing to think of others, who think only of themselves, who don't see their own spiritual poverty. And we are often surprised by those who are considered poor in God's eyes.

For instance, when the ancient city of Sodom comes up in conversation within Christian circles, it is usually in reference to the issue of homosexuality. This is often seen as the central sin of Sodom, the reason why God judged the city. Without denying that issue in the city, we should also take note of Ezekiel 16:49. Ezekiel articulates a different core sin among the people—they didn't aid the poor and needy. The verse says, "Behold, this was the guilt of your sister Sodom: she and her daughters had pride, excess of food, and prosperous ease, but did not aid the poor and needy."

In other words, the people of Sodom were arrogant and selfish. And today, we can be guilty of condemning those "living in sin" while failing to recognize the log in our own eye, that we are just as guilty as those in Sodom in our neglect of the poor. The people of Sodom were arrogant, and their pride was seen in that they had more food than they needed for themselves, yet they didn't reach out and help the disadvantaged. There were people in need around them that they did not help. This was equally offensive to a God who fights for the poor and oppressed.

The people who are for the poor are few.

But Christians should be among these few.

You can be for the poor and not be a follower of Jesus. But you cannot be a true follower of Jesus without being for the poor.

Each gospel writer pens the same story from different angles. Mark tells us the life and ministry of Jesus with a unique focus on his humanity. John writes with a specific conviction that his readers understand that, although Jesus is human, he is in fact God in the flesh. The Scriptures give a well-rounded understanding of the birth, life, ministry, death, and resurrection of Jesus.

Luke's gospel uniquely illuminates Jesus expressing his love toward the poor. Jesus speaks about other things, of course, but a simple reading will show that Luke had a socioeconomic emphasis. Beginning with John the Baptist, the proof of true repentance is economic stewardship in caring for the poor versus extorting them (Luke 3:7–14). As soon as Luke begins to talk about the ministry of Jesus, he makes it clear that Jesus' initial announcement of his ministry was specifically to the poor and oppressed (Luke 4:18–19).

Even Luke's quotations of Jesus draw our attention to the needy state of those whom Jesus came to help. Luke quotes Jesus saying, "Those who are well have no need of a physician, but those who are sick. I have not come to call the righteous but sinners to repentance" (Luke 5:31–32). A sick person knows that he needs help. Jesus came for sick people, people who know they need help.

Luke's gospel is written to evangelize the "rich" and to make sure they know Jesus is the hope for the poor. As a physician, Luke's social sphere was likely among the advantaged of his society, so he writes his gospel to confront and transform his peers. He is reaching out to those like him, those who may not immediately see their need for Jesus, and helping them recognize their need and responsibility to use what they have been given to reach out to those who do not enjoy the ease of life they do. For Luke, following Jesus meant that you generously cared for those in need.

The gospel, according to Luke, turns the more advantaged individual toward the more disadvantaged person.

The Greek term used to describe the "poor" is *ptochos*, and Luke uses this term at least ten times in his gospel. By comparison, Matthew and Mark use it half as much (five times each). For Luke this term first describes those who are disadvantaged economically and materially. The "poor" are, first of all, those who exist in material poverty, a class that is the opposite of the "rich." The term for the rich is *plousis*, and it refers to people consumed by comforts (Luke 8:14) who pursue money as a main priority or safety net in their life (Luke 14:18–24; 16:14). Luke speaks against taking advantage of the poor and neglecting them, whether the neglect is intentional or not.

In Luke's gospel, Jesus doesn't merely issue warnings about taking advantage of the poor. He invites us to join him in loving them and caring for them.

GUILT, DEFLECTION, AND COMPARISON

I have a friend named Rich. He has been everything you would want a friend to be. He is loving and caring, and he speaks truth into my life. We laugh a lot and have cried together through literally some of the toughest times in both of our lives.

When you have friends like this, you learn a lot about one another. You also learn from those who have taught your friends. Rich has a lifelong mentor named Von. And though I've never met Von, his legacy and influence have affected my life through Rich. Von was Rich's youth pastor over fifty years ago. When Rich went to youth group, Von was there to teach him. This youth group was not about lights and lasers, openers and music. Von taught the Scriptures. The kids sang. They had fun.

But they did all these things as they served the poor.

To this day Von still has a ministry in Mexico where he goes five or six days a week and simply provides showers for people living in the city dumps. Some of the people cannot bathe themselves, so Von bathes them. He and his wife have been doing this for decades together.

He sits with the people.

He holds the children.

He laughs with them and teaches them.

He has given his life, literally, to caring for these marginalized people.

Why does he do it?

He says it's because he is a follower of Jesus and that is what Jesus did.

It's that simple for Von.

I'd love to spend a few days with Von. Rich tells me that a day with Von is the closest he has ever gotten to actually walking beside Jesus. For him, those days with Von have brought the heart of God to life. In my own life, I have traveled to over thirty-five countries, many of which have extreme poverty at their core. I have spent time with some amazing people, but Von has become a hero of mine even though we have never met.

I live a thousand miles away from Mexico. There is no place for me to go and bathe people the way Von does. And if I'm not careful, trying to compare myself to Von can make me feel guilty because I'm not doing what he is doing. I think, "I'm not doing enough." So how does someone living a somewhat normal life in the United States embrace Jesus' unique focus on the poor? Is it even possible? How can people who live in the suburbs and work and raise families love the poor the way Jesus did?

Well, let's have an honest talk.

I think it is all too easy for us to overlook poverty camouflaged in a familiar context. We have our ways of driving to work or heading to the grocery store. The streets are familiar. But all too often we drive right by the reality of poverty that surrounds us. People living in the suburbs often don't feel like there is much poverty or homelessness around where they live, so we may justify our lack of engagement with the poor. We do this in very common ways. We talk about the "mission field," but we have in mind everywhere else but where we live. Or we'll talk about missions and donate money, but it's an overseas thing. Or we'll talk about the homeless, but we're primarily thinking of the city, the urban center, not our neighborhood. Missionaries? Those are people who live in Africa or the Middle East. Don't get me wrong. Supporting these people can be a beautiful thing. But here's the problem: if I'm not extremely careful, I unintentionally create a wedge between myself and the place where Jesus has me living every day, and I start to live as though the basic teachings of Jesus don't apply to my life. The truth is that we're all called to be missionaries, right where we live. And we're called to live this way every day.

We look at people like Von as heroes that we can never hope to emulate. We respect the fact that people like Von are doing such things and see it as honorable, but we don't see it in our context. We look to the extreme situations in the world and simply don't see those situations in the community in which we live. Sometimes we just don't *want* to engage.

At other times, it's just that we are ignorant and unaware of the true state of the community we live in. But either way we have excuses that give us a reason not to engage. We talk about how few poor people actually live in our community. We talk about how we need to be "wise" and not enable people to live on the streets. We talk about those that are frauds, panhandling for money because it's easier than getting a real job. We point these types of things out in conversation as if it is an excuse to ignore those with genuine need living among us.

And we also use theological arguments to avoid serving the poor as a lifestyle. Sometimes I hear people who say that helping people is just a "social gospel" that is more concerned about humanitarian needs than proclaiming the gospel. They imply that unless you are continually articulating sin, the cross, and the resurrection every time you feed a hungry person you are somehow not being faithful to Jesus. This mind-set effectively shuts down any hope of engaging God's Spirit in his desire to get us out there serving people in need.

It allows us to stand far from the trenches of loving people and arrogantly point fingers while we, like those in Sodom, feel secure in our comfort.

I don't think most of us consciously do this. Few people will argue against the fact that Jesus had a unique focus on the poor. And many people will even acknowledge that the mission field is all around us. It's anywhere we find ourselves. We believe God has us where we are for a reason. If we don't believe God wants to use us where we live, we need to move. And I also want to be clear that my goal in saying all of this is not to shame you into action. I'm not hoping that you feel bad about yourself and in guilt decide to tutor a student. The Holy Spirit never uses shame as a motivator in our life. When we are being motivated by guilt and shame, it's not the Holy Spirit speaking to us. God invites us to participate in the ways of Jesus, and he motivates us to do this by wowing us with his amazing love for us (2 Corinthians 5:14–15).

Finally, we need to recognize that all of this takes wisdom and discernment as well. There is no magic formula or program to follow in loving and serving the poor. Yes, there are crooked survivalists on the streets that take advantage of those willing to help them, but there are an equal amount of genuine people with needs out there. We need to think wisely then about how we help so that our helping does not hurt those in need. But when in doubt, we should err on the side of helping.

Remember, we aren't doing any of this to earn something from God. You don't earn your salvation. From a biblical perspective, good deeds are evidence that we've been saved—an authentic expression of our salvation. There are a number of ways the Scriptures make this clear. For instance, the apostle Paul was very clear that Titus was to lead people toward doing good works. This would have included caring for other Christians as well as outsiders and in particular the poor and needy. Paul is clear that true salvation leads toward this end (Titus 2:11–14; 3:1–2). Paul says that his exhortation is "trustworthy" and that good works in the life of a believer are necessary (3:8). He even states "devotion" to good works as necessary to avoid unfruitfulness (3:14). And this care and concern for the poor was not unique to Paul. In fact, when the early church leaders met with Paul after his conversion, they told him he was free to do whatever the Lord led him to do, *as long as he continued to care for the poor* (Galatians 2:10). Paul's reply? That was something he was eager to do.

As followers of Jesus, we reflect God's love uniquely toward the poor because of who God is and what he has accomplished through Jesus. It's what Jesus did. If our salvation does not lead us toward the same practical ends as Jesus modeled, something is terribly wrong. And if we value God's Word, we will reflect God's love to people who have less than we do. How we do this matters. We can do it humbly or arrogantly. And sometimes it is hard to tell the difference.

SERVICE AS AN EXERCISE OF GENEROSITY, NOT POWER

Jesus put people and their needs above his own. The cross is evidence of his self-sacrifice. Or you could look at other examples such as when he washed the feet of his followers. Stooping to wash another's feet is an act of humility, something that proclaims value to the other person. It's placing yourself below the other, a humble act that recognizes the dignity of the person being served. And keep in mind that Jesus was not less of a person for doing this. He was and is the Son of God. Humility is not thinking less of ourselves, that we are less valuable or worthless. It is a choice we make to put the needs of others before our own.

In this, our great enemy is selfish pride.

As Westerners, we live in a consumeristic society, and we tend to be very selfish with our perspective on life. We've had individualism ingrained into the fabric of our being. We think about ourselves first and not others. And we often assume that we are always right, that we have rights and deserve certain privileges and comforts. We can barely wrap our minds around the real needs of others because we are very self-centered. We tell ourselves that we need to love ourselves before we can love others. Sounds good, right? Well, that depends on what we really mean. This might just be another self-centered consumer desire. After all, every consumer thinks he or she should come first, before others.

Businesses today refer to something called cultural intelligence. It is knowledge of how to work with diverse people in different cultures. To have cultural intelligence you need to know enough intellectually and relationally about another culture to be able to relate to and work with the people of that culture. Cultural intelligence assumes that you come at another culture from the posture of learning, recognizing that you don't know what you don't know. We need this posture in every relationship in life. We need to learn how to learn about others.

Even more than cultural intelligence we need cultural humility. This is the heart posture in which we approach every relationship with others. We start by viewing others as being more important than we are. Our inborn tendency is to think of ourselves as better than those that have less than we do. We don't even mean it this way. But deep down, we pity them for not having what we have. We see the needs of people more than we see the person behind the need.

But a true understanding of the gospel leads us to humbly offer ourselves for the benefit of others first—specifically the poor. Again, this is about more than giving money. Jesus didn't just meet needs; he generously gave of himself. That's easier said than done for us. It is much easier to fill a kid's backpack once a year than to actually offer ourselves to that child on a daily or weekly basis. In the West, we tend to have excess resources and can be generous without greatly changing our lifestyle. But we aren't truly giving ourselves.

This brings us to an important distinction. It is one thing to become aware of what is going on and what is needed around us (i.e., cultural intelligence), but it is another to follow the ways of Jesus and offer ourselves humbly in a manner that serves and esteems the other (i.e., cultural humility). Pride can motivate us to give of our possessions, but humility is necessary to give of ourselves. Pride denies its own existence, while humility acknowledges itself in caring for the other.

In the following pages my hope is that we'll journey together into several creative and fruitful pathways where we learn some practical and simple ways to offer ourselves as an expression of following Jesus. You may give some money too, and that's great. But most importantly, Jesus calls you to give yourself. Jesus is clear that his life was not about being served, but rather about being a servant of others (Matthew 20:26–28). We miss the idea of generosity because, unlike Jesus, we don't identify ourselves as servants. But if God is by nature selfless and loving . . .

and if Jesus was the perfect imprint of that reality . . .
and if we are followers of Jesus . . .

then we too should offer ourselves to others . . . and especially to the disadvantaged, like he did.

The goal of our serving is for others to experience the love of God in practical ways. Good deeds and serving others communicate God's love nonverbally. Yes, there are times when we will need to use words and communicate God's love that way too. People need to literally hear the truths of Jesus, but nonverbal communication matters too. What we do and the posture in which we do it confirms the truth of the words we speak.

So, I hope that these first chapters have given you a big-picture sense of what Jesus is calling you to do. You may know all of this. Or you may have never thought of any of it before. You may be reading this book thinking, "I just want to learn how to love the kids!" Well, we're getting to that.

If you're like most, you live an arm's length away from people in true need. And this is why I want to tell you some stories of people who have crossed this barrier because of their connection to the local school. These are stories of people who love Jesus and see the school district as a wonderful means for sharing that reality with others. Regardless of where you live . . . I think we can all learn from the stories in the following pages, as we seek to learn how to serve and love people through our local schools.

The How

CHAPTER 4

More than Theory

People often wonder how our church in Portland got so connected to our school district. They assume that it's an anomaly, something that can't be duplicated. They conclude that it could never happen where they live. They can't imagine their church having such an open relationship with the schools in their area.

But remember, I live in Portland. Things like this aren't supposed to happen here. The most important thing to remember is that we all have to start somewhere. I shared a bit about how our relationship began in the first chapter. And today . . . Well, I'll share the words of an employee in our school district who was asked about our partnership and how she felt about it. She said, "I'm terrified to think of the church *not* being involved." And thankfully, we are not the only church serving schools in the Portland metro area.

I think this kind of relationship can and should be

the norm throughout our country and around the world. But in order for this to happen, more Christians need to commit to doing the small things. Take the person whom I just quoted. She was among the most skeptical about working with us when we first started. So how did she end up changing her mind so profoundly? It was the result of a process where Christians did some very simple things that built trust.

And it's not unique to our church in Portland. It's something people are doing all over. Let's look at a few stories to show you what I mean. I'll begin with Sandra. Sandra lives in Fresno, California, and is a mother of four. She started as a volunteer at a Saturday sports program and occasionally helped with an after-school homework club for a school. It was through these opportunities that she began to become aware of growing needs. She also got to know some key people around the schools and school district. It's amazing what happens when you are simply around and available!

Sandra slowly started to become known in the community and at the school. After some time of volunteering at the school herself, she discovered a neighborhood thrift store that was started by some people from The Well, a church in her city. Sandra started volunteering at the thrift shop from time to time. She eventually became employed as the coordinator of the

thrift store warehouse. Because of her existing relationships with school district employees, she is now able to
provide a practical bridge for families in need as well as
provide a bridge for others that want to help the disadvantaged families that have children going to a school
in the district.

And it all started with a decision to volunteer from
time to time on Saturdays.

Sandra didn't start out with a grand plan. She offered
herself and did one thing, and then God took care of
the rest. It started with participation and presence—one
individual who was doing something to help. It led to
additional forms of service in which she could continue
giving herself to others. In her case, it eventually turned
into a full-time job.

At our church, Colossae, in Portland, it's nearly
impossible for us to separate the stories of our involvement with the local school district from our work with
families in need. When we first started to connect with
schools, we asked them what the biggest need in the
community was. Their response was unanimous: homeless students and their families. Many didn't even have
family in the area. This was communicated as the high-
est priority by both the school district *and* the police
department.

But let's be honest. That is a huge thing to tackle.

We didn't know where to start. Honestly, we didn't do much at all in this area for the first few years. Instead, we focused on doing one thing well. We provided an employee to the school district who volunteered in the resource center. The people of our church volunteered in very simple ways around the schools. We knew that the needs were vast, as they are at any school. All you have to do is ask and look a little deeper.

So we were caught off guard a bit when we first heard that the biggest issue needing to be tackled was homeless youth. We would never have guessed it! But once again, this was a reality check for us. We weren't as aware of the true needs in our community until we got intimately connected to the school district in our area. We became aware of the greater needs because we offered ourselves to do the small things first.

Ally Kinnaman is on staff with us full time at Colossae and serves as the liaison between our church and the school district. A couple of years ago, we led an effort together with her and a few other key volunteers to start a more structured program to help with the overwhelming homeless needs that Ally was in touch with while working at our school district's resource center.[2] The majority of the kids in need are unaccompanied teens, without a nurturing adult in their life. The first teen Ally helped out with our new effort was a teenager I'll call Stephanie.[3]

"Stephanie's story is one that demonstrates what is possible when ordinary people within the body of Christ decide to step into the messiness of life with one who is hurting. In my opinion, it is the most profound demonstration of Jesus' love that we can show to another."

—*Ally Kinnaman*

When Ally first met Stephanie, Stephanie was fifteen years old and living in a trailer with an unrelated family. Due to the large number of people living in this confined space, Stephanie could only stay with this family for a short time. Often she was in a situation where she had literally nowhere to go. Her mom had been deported to Mexico, and her father had moved back to Mexico as well.

Stephanie was failing all of her classes, she was chronically absent, and she had learned that she was going to have to retake her freshman year of high school. The odds were stacked against her in almost every way.

Ally was able to get Stephanie placed with a Christian family who welcomed her into their home like a daughter. They loved her and made the extra effort necessary to help her in school and in her personal life. Amazingly, Stephanie passed all of her classes that year and was able to stay on track with her studies. Although the original plan we discussed was for temporary placement, the family has become so close with Stephanie that they plan to house her until she goes off to college.

As wonderful as that story is, it doesn't end there! You see, Stephanie has an eighteen-year-old sister I'll call Madison.

"I was sixteen [at the time], overwhelmed and feeling broken. Through the choices that I made and those who chose to get involved, I now have a relationship with Jesus, stability within a family, and a community of people who love me."

—*Madison*

Like her sister, Madison was about to lose her current living situation. She was staying with a single mom of two who was living in a tiny apartment. Instead of attending school, Madison spent her days working at Taco Bell. She had an eighth-grade education level. Through Ally and our new program reaching out to homeless youth, Madison was placed with two single women from our church. They were in their twenties at the time, so it wasn't a traditional family setting; but these two younger ladies wanted to express God's love by caring for someone in need. The young women instantly embraced Madison as a sister. They helped her enroll in an alternative school track instead of having to re-enroll in traditional high school where she would be four years behind.

These girls are also volunteers in a ministry called Young Life. There are dozens of Young Life leaders in our church, and it's a wonderful thing to have so many adults focused on reaching out to teenagers. These are our "youth workers." Because of her relationship with these women who took her in, Madison naturally got involved with Young Life and ended up giving her life to Christ at summer camp. Still, as helpful as these young ladies were to Madison, it eventually became clear to everyone that it would be a better long-term situation for Madison to move in with a traditional family where she could have parental figures in her life.

A family from our church took her in, and as I write they plan for Madison to stay with them indefinitely. Despite living with different families, Madison and Stephanie are actually closer now as biological sisters and have a healthier relationship than they ever have before. I see them in church just about every single week. Their family is being mended through the hospitality and simple willingness of other families to share themselves. It's a beautiful thing to see!

To have people like this in our church is an honor.

It's humbling to be around such servants.

We've learned that it really doesn't take that much to have an impact.

It just takes starting somewhere.

Be aware that not all of our stories end in permanent

placement. Sometimes, a family simply needs assistance for a season while they get back on their feet. This was the case for a young single mother living in downtown Portland who was putting herself through school while working full time. She found herself often needing to sleep at work and had no furniture in the home where she and her five-year-old daughter lived. Knowing this situation was not sustainable for her or her child, she reached out for a helping hand. A family at Colossae allowed her daughter to live with them for six weeks. During this time, they stepped up to help furnish her apartment and give her the tools she needed to get her life into a more manageable situation.

At the end of six weeks, she was able to bring her daughter home to a more livable apartment. The family that helped her continues to babysit for free on a weekly basis. In fact, we recently had the family over for a Saturday morning breakfast when this beautiful little girl was staying the weekend with them. As is often the case, the family that stepped up to help in this situation was so energized by the experience that they now are involved in many other opportunities through the school district. For example, this Thanksgiving they rallied the people in their Colossae community to put together twenty-five food baskets for families in need. Again, it's a simple thing to do, but over time these authentic expressions of love speak loudly to civic leaders.

And when a bunch of people are doing simple things, it often has a way of becoming personal.

I remember a call we got from an elementary school counselor. He had a family that was homeless. My wife and I talked about it, and we decided to help. I initially went to meet the family—like I often do—with one or all of my children. This time I had brought along my oldest daughter, Karis, who was ten years old at the time.

When we pulled up to meet this struggling family of five, they were all sitting in a truck. The counselor introduced me to the parents and then to the children. We talked about their situation—their immediate needs—and we got them food and arranged a place for them to sleep.

During our time with this family, I could tell that Karis was really hitting it off with one of the children. After we left, Karis told me that their daughter was in her class at school. Up until this point Karis had no idea of her friend's situation. This was yet another reminder that our kids can form friendships at school that they might not make elsewhere. This was a great moment for Karis and me to talk honestly about the difficulties of people who lived around us, the challenges and struggles they were facing, how we could help, and why we should.

As amazing as that opportunity was with my daughter, the crazy thing is that this was not the only time this has happened. Time after time we've been in a position to help the family of a classmate without knowing it ahead of time. And each time this has happened, it's been a great chance to talk with our children. They often had no idea their classmates were in such need.

Sometimes you just need to offer yourself to see what the needs are.

"We always felt like the extra space in our home over the years could be put to better use than as a guest room or office. Bringing Kenzie into our home and family has certainly changed her life and transformed ours as well. We have learned that there are real, desperate needs all around us that can be met by letting the Lord use your life and home."

—*Family from Colossae*

It's easy to think of broken or "poor" families with children under eighteen needing help. But what about those kids once they're out of high school and on their own? Kenzie came from a "poor" home situation. Both parents were alcoholics, and Kenzie was essentially parenting her own mom. She paid all the bills while she tried to guide her mom to sobriety. Kenzie was known as a hard worker and was attending a local community college on full scholarship while she tried to take care of things at home. Her mom had recently come into some money through Social Security, and while you'd think that would have improved Kenzie's situation, it did quite the opposite. Her mom told her that she didn't want her around anymore now that she had access to funds of her own, and Kenzie was turned out of the house and left with her dog and all of her possessions inside her car.

She was living like this until a family from Colossae took Kenzie into their home. The original plan was for Kenzie to stay with them for the summer, but they have settled in so well that she stayed through that school year and has no plans of leaving until graduation.

Kenzie grew up without much exposure to church or the influence of faith and is now taking time to really wrestle through that area of her life. She attends our church with her host family, and it's safe to say that she would not be in this situation if it weren't for followers of Jesus expressing God's love by giving her the practical help she needed. They first shared the gospel with her through their actions and have now earned the right to share it with their words. They are having wonderful conversations about who Jesus is and what he has done.

SMALL THINGS MATTER

I realize that most of the stories I've shared involve a family taking in another child to live with them. And for many people that is intimidating. Some people just are not in a position to serve in that way. But don't feel guilty. I wanted to give you a small picture of what is possible if Christians give themselves. There's an abundance of other ways to be involved.

For example, through our connection with schools, one community in our church met a family living in their car. Their eight-year-old daughter attends a local elementary school and had contracted a bladder infection due to her inability to shower. The Colossae community who met this family gathered some money and purchased a pass to a local swim center so that the family had access to showers. They also paid for the gas they needed to move their car to a better location.

Purchasing some swim passes and filling up a gas tank may not be what you would picture when you think about helping the poor. Yet that's exactly what was needed in this specific situation. Sometimes we have to let go of the ways we envision ourselves helping in order to actually improve someone's life and solve their immediate need. This community group simply met the need, blessed the family, and that was the end of the relationship. Every small thing can lead to a meaningful relationship. We have to be okay with this sort of ending. It's a reality at times.

We have to get out of our own way and humbly and happily be willing to meet a need instead of being disappointed that we weren't able to serve in an extravagant way with a great ending to the story. Needs come in all shapes and sizes, and we need to stay flexible and alert if we want to remain effective. Not everything we do pays off as a sermon illustration or a story written about in a book. But that's never been the point anyway.

The point is to have a faithful presence in our community as God's people.

We cannot control every result, but we can all do something.

We hope for specific fruitful outcomes, but we only need to measure our own obedience.

We can all offer ourselves in some way.

Have you ever tried to walk around in shoes that are too small for you? Even if they pinch or rub only slightly, it has to be one of the most distracting and annoying feelings in the world. There is a teenage boy who attends high school in our neighborhood and wears size 14 shoes. For many of us, finding shoes of that size would simply be an inconvenience, but for this boy's family it was impossible. They were hard to find and too expensive to obtain. As a result, he had to walk around wearing shoes that were *two sizes* too small for him. Think about the impact that would have on a teenager . . . The discomfort of every step reminding you of the helplessness you feel in your situation, the embarrassment of classmates noticing that you can't afford shoes that fit you properly . . .

A family in our church heard about this need and *immediately* went out and purchased him a decent pair of Nikes. Now that young man can walk his school halls with the confidence that he will not be distracted by the pain or embarrassment his feet had caused him.

My point is that when you have a bunch of people doing a bunch of little things like this, you begin to collectively have an impact in a community. One group in our church spent an entire afternoon cleaning all the bleachers in the football stadium so that they would look nice for graduation. Now, I don't know that anyone sat in those bleachers and thought, "Wow, these are so clean. Someone who loves Jesus must have really invested time into this community." But it is exactly this kind of service, the tasks that are appreciated by few, that Jesus calls us to perform. Additionally, there are those who notice. Gus, the high school janitor, noticed for sure. We approach Gus often to find out what we can do to help him. The teachers will notice. Sometimes, those in administration notice.

What do they notice?

The fact that a group of people who love Jesus are willing to help and do the small things.

They notice the fact that people took a Saturday afternoon to do something that gets zero praise but helps the administration do their job more effectively.

They notice that these people come from one church which happens to have a lot of other people doing small things too.

It's the snowball effect.

We will talk more about this type of strategy later, but my point here is that you don't need to dream up a grand plan or an amazing strategy to change your community. In fact, it is often the unappreciated tasks done in humility and out of love that earn the most trust over time. No one has cause to question your motives for helping in these small ways. This isn't just my opinion. A Portland city employee who runs the resource center has said that they often get people who come with a desire to serve, but they will specify the specific ways in which they are willing to help. This can become a burden because it forces the city employees to do extra work to find a need or project that fits the specific desire of the volunteer. In contrast, they find it incredibly refreshing to have volunteers from the church come and ask to meet *whatever* needs they can, regardless of how menial the tasks may seem.

This kind of service removes all pride or self-glorification from the equation.

These types of things build trust with members of a community.

We become known, simply, as servants.

Sounds like Jesus to me.

CHOOSE COMMUNITY OVER INDIVIDUALISM, ALWAYS

Another helpful guard against pride is collaborating with others to meet a need none of us could meet on our own. This protects us from the individualism that often creeps into our Western mind-set. You may have noticed that a lot of stories in this chapter talked about a Colossae community rallying in our church and meeting a need together. While there are individuals doing wonderful things on their own or as a family, most of our partnership with the school district works because people are joining hand in hand to get it done instead of trying to tackle it on their own.

One example of this is a family who was about to be evicted from their apartment because they couldn't pay their rent that month. This family knew they had a paycheck coming that would allow them to pay in the subsequent months. If their record was marred with an eviction before then, it would be incredibly difficult for them to find any other apartment that would accept them. A school counselor brought this to the attention of one of our Colossae community leaders. While no single person or family in that group had enough funds to cover the rent, the community group as a whole came together and contributed the necessary money to keep that family in their apartment. There was no need for the money to come out of a church budget line because there was a community of people that owned the need themselves.

Another local family had their power shut off during a cold Oregon winter. A different community group pulled together their resources to get that family back into a heated home. I've heard story after story like this, where a group of people in our congregation pulls together to meet a daunting need. The community group my family is part of has taken on the task of caring for a family living in a terrible environment. We rallied to pay for and physically repair their trailer in a number of ways. I'm sure many more innovative solutions have happened in our church that I have no idea about.

In Christian circles, creating unity and community among their congregation is something pastors and leaders are constantly working toward. Too often, in an attempt to create unity, effort and energy are solely poured *into* the church instead of being poured *out* of the church. The leaders begin to focus "inside" the church rather than focusing on getting people to rally outside, together. Community with other Christians is often held up as the end goal for people as if all Jesus wants us to have is a safe place to hang out with other Christians. Believe it or not, community is actually *not* an end we should pursue. Christian community is a means for loving and serving others. It is a perfect means for reflecting God as a loving relationship!

Another way of saying this is that as the church we must see ourselves as a collective group created for the purpose of reaching out together (Matthew 5:14–16). We are people on a mission together, and what we do together speaks into a community in ways that people hanging out with each other in Bible studies does not. Bible study and small groups are needed in the church. But they are a means to an end, not the goal we seek. It may sound counterintuitive, but we have had far more success in bringing the body together by getting people to think about what they can do together out in the community. This outward focus has increased fruitful fellowship between Christians in our church so much more than internally focused groups.

There is a time and a place for building up the body internally, and at Colossae we call this being the "body to the body." It comes from Romans 12:5 where Paul calls Christians members of the body of Christ. We talk about serving and caring for one another, learning about and from Jesus together, praying for one another to become more like him, and finally encouraging and exhorting one another toward the ways of Jesus.

But these expressions of being the "body to the body" happen organically when we are being the "body to the world." There are a few reasons for this. When we practice a lifestyle of service, we are necessarily in community with others or we burn out and quit our "good works" after becoming isolated and exhausted. When we partner in service with others, we have someone to share in the joy and burdens of the experience. We have others to lean on when our own humanity requires us to take a step back and rest. A lifestyle of serving others is also bound to be a little messy. A solitary life might be neat, but it is not fruitful. Instead, we must learn to organize ourselves around reaching and serving others.

I've come to realize we cannot be selfish and make disciples.

I've seen this reality lived out in our church. Many individuals are giving some time to tutoring kids or volunteering weekly in the office at a school. Many families are taking on foster children through the Department of Health and Human Services or helping families in need through our relationship with the school district. Other families are stepping up to be "respite families" where they can provide childcare when foster parents need a weekend off. Still others who are in a community group with those housing children have stepped up and offered to help cover the costs of caring for these individuals. Nothing brings people together quite like mutually caring for children in need of a loving home. When we start caring for God's children together, we experience what it means to be God's family.

And we become a family that others want to belong to.

These relationships have developed over time. But one of the first things we organized as a church wasn't a formal program to care for families in crisis; it was a service event where we spread bark dust on an elementary school playground. We had to start somewhere!

As we move into the next chapter, we will look at some creative ways to engage and get started. Remember, you don't need to tackle the big problems head on—and certainly not right away. Start with something simple, something you can do. And build from that.

CHAPTER 5

BEING CREATIVE

Creativity is the crazy reality in which something new and valuable is formed. Ideas are shared—both the possible and the seemingly impossible. New dreams and visions emerge in multiple forms, as part of a bedtime story, a joke, or even a musical composition. Creativity takes on physical forms like paintings, poems, or projects. Often associated with certain personality traits or specific environments, at heart it is about making something better or developing something entirely new.

Some people are wired for creativity. Others prefer to take hold of something already in place and run with it. Some people envision a new possibility and build it. Others have a hard time articulating what they see, even if they feel the need. And some are simply more creative than others. Yet as far back as the Garden of Eden narrative, we see that every person is hard-wired for creativity. It's in our DNA. We all have thoughts and ideas to make the world a better place.

Creativity is motivated by something within us. Something inside pushes us toward new things. Some of us tend to have a lot of energy. Others are contemplators, brilliant and full of new and fresh ideas. Some are motivated toward creativity out of an embedded need to communicate new things to others. They are communicators by nature, having an inward need to stimulate others by causing them to think about new things.

Seeing needs often gives birth to creativity. People like this aren't necessarily inventors—they are problem solvers. They live in the trenches of everyday life, feel the tensions of the real world, and see problems that need to be solved. These creative types tend to stumble onto ideas or develop them through trial and error.

Creativity can take many forms.

Recognizing that we all have creative ideas that are expressed in different ways helps us when we think about working with public schools. Working with schools takes some creativity, no doubt! Every school has different leaders with different obstacles and opportunities. This chapter lets you in on some of the creative ideas that have proven effective in serving schools. My hope is that these stories will inspire creativity in your own setting. Of course, you may try to implement some of the ideas found in this chapter, but my hope is that you'll create some of your own. Either way, I want to catapult you into a deeper and more fruitful relationship with your local schools.

Some of the ideas may seem too difficult for you to

implement. Don't let that scare you away! I want to give you a broad picture of what others are doing in the hope that it will get some creative juices flowing so that you can find something effective for your context. Know in advance that some of these ideas won't fit you—your personality, giftedness, or passions. That is okay too. It's frustrating to try to be someone else. So be encouraged as you read these stories. Celebrate with those who are seeing fruit come from their creativity.

On the other hand, you may see some of these ideas and think to yourself, "These are trivial" or "I've seen that a hundred times." You might even think a few are a bit cheesy. You might be able to poke holes in the idea and describe ten reasons why this would not work where you live. But none of that is beneficial, and it certainly won't help you to be creative in your own context. The point is not for you to shoot these ideas down but to celebrate the diverse ways that followers of Christ are stepping up, taking initiative, and doing something to serve the local schools where they live.

The rest of this chapter will be broken up into three major sections. First, I will share about some projects that we've tried. These tend to be one-time or short-term events. Second, we'll look at some long-term programs that have been started. Finally, I will share some initiatives people are engaging with that build trust over time. Not everyone can run a program or organize and manage group projects. However, everyone can do something for someone else in some practical way, so that's what we will end the chapter with.

PROJECT IDEAS

What's the difference between a project and a program? Well, in the way I'm using it, I think of a project as a one-time event or something that has a limited time frame. This might be a single-day work project or an event that you host. Some of these things will likely be familiar to you, but I am also confident there will be some new ideas as well. Remember that these are starting points, not end goals. There are many churches and individuals doing projects at schools. However, few view these projects as part of a bigger picture. This chapter is not intended to create a pressure release valve, where people do something because they feel guilty for not engaging. One-time service events do not define what it means to follow Jesus. Rather, as followers of Jesus, service is our way of life. So as I share, it is important to see these as the types of things serving as a means to a greater relational end.

When viewed as part of the larger picture, one-time projects can be very beneficial.

They help the church to be seen as a resource.

They help us articulate the servant mentality and life of Jesus.

They give us reasons to share why we are doing what we are doing.

We can meet some very practical needs.

They are a practical means for building trust with decision makers who have the capability of opening other doors that can lead to a long-term and fruitful relationship. When we offer ourselves humbly as a resource to help meet the most pressing needs with no other strings attached, we build trust and build relationships. Here are some project ideas you might consider organizing— whether with friends, your small group, or with your church as a whole as a trust-building platform.

Facility Upkeep and Maintenance

There is bark to be spread, play structures to be built, painting to be done. Gym floors need to be refinished, football fields need landscaping, and tracks need to be installed. There are always work projects for which volunteer manpower is appreciated. Not everything needs to be done as an all-church event. You can walk to the front office of any school, introduce yourself, and volunteer your services. You can even suggest a couple of contractors you know who'd like to get involved. You can identify parts of the campus that you've noticed need attention and offer yourself as a resource to help. We will talk about the key people to connect with in the next chapter. But know that these one-time work projects can be a tremendous front door to a sustainable relationship.

The First Day of School

There is always a lot of energy and synergy on the first day of school. People are excited to see others and are in a social mind-set. Recognize this as the perfect time to reach out and offer your help. For instance, one group of people purchased coffee mugs with the high school's logo on one side and "WELCOME BACK!" on the other. This group handed out fresh hot coffee in the mugs to every teacher and administrator who walked through the door. It was a simple way to be present in an encouraging way. And it was a creative way of participating in the natural flow of what the school was already doing. Far too often we offer ourselves only if it fits what we are doing. However, it is often much more effective to find creative ways to join in with and actively participate in what is already happening at the schools.

Personalize School Environments

Another idea is to take a general gathering place for teachers or administrators and personalize it a bit. For instance, most schools have some sort of teachers' lounge. It's a place for teachers to go where they don't have to be "on." They can relax and be called by their first names.

We've had people personalize these places with paint, pillows, and pictures. Schools usually don't have much budget to make these environments comfortable. One family took the initiative to organize a makeover of the teachers' lounge. They made it personal by obtaining pictures of the children of teachers and administrators and then hung them all along one wall in the room. They also organized a contest where other teachers had to match the children with the appropriate parent. The winner received a $100 gift card to Target. It was a fun way of participating in a relational way at the school. You can do something similar with coaches' offices or the office area where counselors work.

Annual Events

Every year schools host annual events like carnivals, plays, choir concerts, and more. One group offered themselves as a cleaning crew after shows. They cleaned and organized the theater dressing room before and after shows, helped clean instruments for kids, and hung up the band uniforms after a Friday night football game. This group wanted to help serve those involved in the arts at the school, but their ideas can apply to other areas as well. Any one of these things may not have a huge citywide impact in themselves. But when you have multiple groups of people doing something like this on a campus, things begin to change!

PROGRAM IDEAS

When I say programs, I'm referring to concepts with an ongoing structure and schedule that are organized to help address systemic problems within a community. Because programs are ongoing, they require more work and commitment and typically need a dedicated leader. They also tend to be more sustainable, both relationally and economically, because they draw a deeper level of commitment than a one-time event. They are not easily developed or thrown together, and because of this, most people are reluctant to start a new one. But don't let that intimidate you.

Some of the best programs are developed out of relationship, and they are also a means for building relationships. Someone typically has a heart to address a tension or a problem and then goes about organizing it one step at a time. The nice thing about a program is that once you've started it and it has proven effective in one context, it may be adapted to other contexts as well. Following are a few examples.

Medical/Dental Programs

I wrote a bit about this in chapter 1 and have included more details in Appendix B that you can reference if you'd like to do something like this yourself. The program we organize began as a one-time event but has since turned into a series of ongoing clinics. This kind of commitment requires ongoing organization and funding.

The program we started has helped relieve the resource center for the school district by providing a solution to the immediate health needs of underinsured families within the district. In recent years, some of the medical needs have been decreasing as families have signed up for subsidies for health insurance, but the dental needs are still vast. And other specialties such as podiatry and vision care are not typically covered by medical insurance, so those needs still need to be addressed. Our clinics play a small part in partnering with the schools to meet these needs.

Relational Teams

You might consider pulling together teams of parents, former students, professionals, and business owners to work with overburdened counselors in the schools, especially those working at the high school level. This team can work alongside the counselors to offer classes on applying for college scholarships or on filling out college applications. Or the team can work with them to put together parent Q&A sessions. We have seen these programs attract families that are not well educated and who desire a better education for their children. The post–high school process is daunting to say the least, especially for parents who don't have any experience in navigating that world. The needs can be bigger than you realize, so you might want to start out just offering courses for freshmen. I know that sounds backwards, but if you want to make a sustainable and long-term difference, it is best to get the families of freshmen thinking ahead as soon as possible. This will make any future work you do with juniors and seniors much easier.

Another idea is to pull together teams of adult volunteers that coordinate themselves to go and watch certain sports games and activities. Some will go to the home baseball games, others to football or volleyball. They are a cheering section to encourage the student athletes. Many groups have focused on less attended sports. For example, in some schools wrestling meets are well attended, but in others hardly so. Girls' basketball might be the strongest sport or perhaps the opposite at a certain school. Regardless of the context, there are teams and coaches that would love a little extra encouragement from a group of people who "adopt" their team to cheer for.

AmeriCorps Jobs

I will take a closer look at the laws separating state and church in the coming pages, but we should acknowledge that there are inherent fears on both sides of the fence. There are some teachers and administrators who are more cautious about having individual Christians or Christian organizations (such as churches) directly involved in a program at their school. This can be frustrating when all you want to do is help. Options like AmeriCorps can create an alternative. If there is a need at a school, but you find they are extremely cautious about working with a church, consider developing a job description and apply through AmeriCorps for the position you create. You can then let the administrator know that the church is funding it. This protects the administrator if there are tensions he or she faces about your program. AmeriCorps is something worth considering for a number of reasons, but cost is certainly among those. The program itself provides most of the funding. A church can even choose the AmeriCorps member (i.e., employee) that will run the program that is developed for the school. This is an effective way we began to build trust with the schools in our area. But I'm getting ahead of myself. More on this option later.

Third-Space Environments Well & Good Coffee House is the name of a coffee shop our church launched in partnership with two foundations. Today, many churches have what are referred to as "third-place" environments where people can meet informally. For our church, the coffee shop is a means to meet needs in our community that complements the work we are doing with our school district.

We originally started the coffee house to meet needs in the community, and having the coffee shop separate from our church building and next to hundreds of businesses allows for us to run something within the community that isn't explicitly "Christian." Rather, it is a place where families, students, and individuals from every domain of society can come. We run it on a nonprofit basis, not taking any money from the business. The church gives 100 percent of the shop's surplus toward meeting needs in the community. We don't advertise it this way though, because such a label seems to make people assume the coffee and food are bad.

The school district loves the coffee house, and teachers and administrators often tell people to go there because they know how much we are able to help others. These types of social businesses can be complex to get started—we know that. They take strong leadership and financing to get off the ground. But if they are successful, they can be a powerful funding source and a fruitful ministry.

Staffing Assistance

We are especially excited when we can supply actual, full-time employees for a school. Drawing from things like the funding provided by the coffee house, we have been able to provide several employees for a junior high in our area, the high school in our city, and even in the school district offices.

We currently have an employee that works in the resource center where teachers and counselors refer families in need. Although this employee is a church staff member, she has a district email address, a district badge, and is seen and valued as a district employee. This is yet another way in which credibility and trust is built over time.

We started by spreading bark on a playground, did one thing after another to build relationships over time, and now we are able to work together in more significant and relational ways. Not all churches are able to fund full-time employees, but even if that's not an option, you can still adopt a school and do a number of service-oriented projects to build a fruitful relationship. Other schools have funded part-time employees to serve in roles such as community liaison or volunteer coordinator. One of our employees had a desk among the counselors at the high school, and whenever there was a practical need that came up, she was notified. She would bring that need to the community leaders within our church, and the need would quickly be met.

None of these programs are perfect. They all take time and effort to get off the ground, but they can be simple, strategic, and effective on a number of different levels. The bottom line is that programs like these provide a sustainable and ongoing solution for problems the school is, for whatever reason, not able to address.

PEOPLE IDEAS

You've probably guessed this already, but the best asset you can offer a school is not a program or a project—it's people. As we discussed in the first two chapters, there is something wonderful that happens when we simply offer ourselves. This is what Jesus did, and it is very effective in showing his love to others. There will always be financial and facility needs. But there's something special about an individual walking into the front office and simply saying they want to volunteer their time as a member of the community.

We recently had a member of one of our church plants do this. She simply walked into the school's front office and said that she lived in the community and wanted to help. Surprisingly, they told her nobody had ever done that before. They said to her, "Well, we're not sure what to do with that because nobody has ever offered to help like you have." Amazing. She has persistently offered herself for anything they need: answering phones, stuffing envelopes, whatever comes up. She is retired and she sees the school district as a means for her to be connected to the core of her community. The relationship is slow moving, but it is growing, and she is earning trust through her gentle persistence. That's just one example. There are a number of different ways individuals can get involved and participate in helping meet needs.

Here is a list of things you might consider:

- Coach a sport or run a theater program.
- Offer to volunteer answering the phone a couple of hours a week. Teachers are often on a rotation for things like this, and some have to give up their "prep" period to do this. Your help can free up those teachers and give you a consistent presence in the school.
- Tutor a kid or two or three. Every school has kids in dire need of someone who cares. This is also a fantastic connection with the families of students.
- Join a team. Become a member of groups such as the PTA or sit on the school's site council. These committees provide meaningful connections

with parents and other community members. My wife is the PTO secretary, and I sit on the site council of our daughters' school. It's a wonderful way that we as parents can be a resource.

- Go to school board meetings. You can give your input as well as get an inside view of how the school board makes decisions that affect your community's schools.
- Get technical. If you have some sort of skill set in technology, offer your assistance. There is always a need for computer skills, website help, and even help with the school network administration.
- Drive places. Teachers are always in need of parents to chaperone field trips.
- Volunteer with a teacher. Teachers do a lot more than just teach kids. There is a ton of organization necessary, tests and homework to be graded, and a number of other things that require the teacher's time.
- Volunteer at the school library. Most schools are short on funding to pay someone to run their library, so they rely on volunteer help to keep the library open for students. Offer to check out books for people or stock them. Assist students or even offer to donate money for some needed books.

LAST THOUGHTS

All of the things I have mentioned here are simple ideas, but they take creativity and some effort to make them work. Remember that the project or program is not the goal. It's a means to an end—showing God's love to those at the core of our community. We do that by following Jesus in the giving of ourselves. Because public schools usually have their fingers on the pulse of the community, if you start out by asking what they need, you'll likely find ways you can assist. And my guess is that you'll enjoy it! The people I know who are involved find it to be fun, joyful, and a fantastic way to gain friends they would never have met otherwise. Sitting on the site council of an elementary school, I have been overwhelmingly pleased by my interactions with the teachers and seeing how much they truly love their students.

By being involved in these ways, we gain credibility and trust, both as individuals and as a church community. We also gain insight into how people are devoting their lives, what they care about, and what frustrates them. The principal of the school my daughters attend, Mr. Blasquez, is a wonderful man who loves his job and truly wants what is best for the kids attending his school. I know this because he has taken the time to sit down with me over lunch and to share his vision for the school. As a parent, I am excited to help him achieve that vision. He is even helping us achieve ours. He is not a Christian but recently joined me in all our church services. I interviewed him about the growing needs in the schools. It was a wonderful time! You see, over time, opportunities arise to share why we are involved. And when this happens in the context of a relationship, it's a powerful testimony to God's love.

In the next chapter, we want to look at ways you can be strategic in your planning. There are certain employees of the schools and district that can accomplish more than others. And while we want to love those in need, we also need to understand that some people can get things done better than others. These are strategic people to build relationships with, and in the next chapter we will discuss how to effectively develop those.

Everyone can have impact when they are intentional.

CHAPTER 6

BEING STRATEGIC

There's a simple truth I've fully embraced: relationships matter.

Relationships are critical to everyday life . . . and to professional success. People refer people they know and will often hire them as well. On the other hand, relationships can sometimes narrow our thinking and lead to bias. If a coach in the National Football League knows a particular agent really well, he is more likely to give that agent's athlete an opportunity before others represented by someone he doesn't know. This leads to another truth about how life works.

Trust is relationally driven. This means that opportunities are often gained or lost based on who knows whom and how well they know them. We don't have to like this reality, but we can't ignore it.

To this point, we've looked at stories of people who have done some amazing things. We have talked about projects and programs that have had a sustainable impact. But without relationships those things would have never happened.

Somebody knew someone.

Trust was built in some way.

Most programs start local. They grow and maybe they become nationally recognized. They come to be seen as trusted organizations, and that is often because reputations are built on the foundation of healthy relationships. At the end of chapter 5, we talked about a number of ways in which any individual can get involved at a local school. These are simply ways to become known and trusted. Everyone starts somewhere. We spread bark dust to meet a need. We clean a bathroom. We serve a cup of coffee or give out a water bottle at a sports game. We do it to serve but also in hope of building long-term trust. This is especially true with decision makers.

To be clear, we're not talking about a bait-and-switch technique. If you try to use or manipulate people with an ulterior motive, they will see through it. And that has nothing to do with the love of Christ. There are some things we do just because they need to be done. There is goodness in bark spreading, even if no relationships result from it. We are not looking to force some sort of "pitch" for Jesus. We are simply trying to be who we are: image bearers committed to reflecting the loving God we worship through all our deeds. But we will also pray and hope for long-term relationships that will prove to be fruitful. We will hope and pray through everything we do!

You might refer to it as strategy.

You see, it's not just about who you know.

It's also a matter of who knows you.

Meeting practical needs such as spreading mulch at an elementary playground or helping a school plant a garden are helpful ways to become known. We offer ourselves as a resource by volunteering, and over time we gain a reputation as trusted people. As Christians we want to be known as people who care, who offer ourselves, and who reach out to those in need. But that doesn't mean we should avoid thinking wisely and being strategic in what we do. So building on the foundation we've laid already, this chapter is all about being strategic in what you do. Think about the bigger picture. You may need to do some investigating, learning how things work in your community and in your school district. You will want to know who holds the keys to doors you'd like to open and how to develop meaningful relationships with those folks so you aren't constantly banging your head against a wall.

But there is one caution I want to add before we identify these people.

NO BLANKET FORMULA

Remember that there are differing philosophies and theories on how to do just about everything. Coaches have a variety of different approaches. Parenting philosophies vary greatly. Churches embrace different models and methodologies. But these differences don't necessarily mean one way is universally right and others are wrong. Some parents homeschool, others prefer their children to attend private schools, and others want their children to be in the public school system. "Biblical" reasons can be given in support of each conviction.

Most churches have some sort of "small group" environment that they promote to one degree or another. However, the methods and emphases of these groups can be vastly different. Some think cell groups are best and have articulated their reasons for holding firmly to that model, while others have reasons why they believe cell groups are entirely ineffective. Some churches are centered around missional communities, while others are centered around content studies such as Bible studies or Sunday school classes. And then there are churches that are a hybrid of different models.

Anything that requires leadership will also have differing opinions by those who lead; they will each have a way of going about what they do. Every leader will (or at least should) have reasons why they do specific things and reasons why they don't do others. It's important to understand this as we approach working with schools and school districts.

There is no blanket formula applied to every school.

They all do things differently, and it takes time to learn those ways.

So we need to talk about *words* and *models*. These must be at the forefront of our minds, because they significantly impact how we will relate to people within these organizations.

The first thing is recognizing the fact that words carry different connotations for different people. For instance, when someone talks about "disciplining" their children, some people think about spanking. Others may believe spanking is wrong, and they have an entirely different picture of what that looks like. So a word like *discipline* plays out differently for different people. Another example is a term like *community group*. One person might think of a group of people that gather and study the Bible together. Another person thinks of a group of people sharing a weekly meal together. These connotations vary based on their personal experience.

As I write this, I'm currently visiting Amsterdam, Netherlands. Words are different here. Coffee shops are not what they are in the United States. You can find them, but here "coffee shops" are places to buy marijuana, hash, or alcohol. If you are in Amsterdam and want to go to a coffee place like the ones you would find in the U.S., you are better off going to a "bar." That's the name of the place where coffee is served.

Why does this matter? Because when we approach a

relationship with a school district, we must be careful to avoid assuming that we understand what is being said and that we are communicating what we intend to communicate. You may use familiar words (such as job titles), but that doesn't mean you and they are talking about the same position. More on that later.

Second, we need to realize that the words we use can carry baggage. People have convictions, and those convictions sometimes carry through in strong opinions about what should and should not be done. You may be a parent who has the conviction to send your children to public school and might believe that it's "more biblical" to have your kids go to a school where there is a high percentage of poor families present. I have heard parents say they want to raise their children "in the world" so they can personally walk them through the tension of being in it. But this becomes problematic when parents think the way they do things is *the* right way or even the *only* way to raise children. Strong opinions are one thing, but when we try to force them upon others, it can damage newly forming relationships. This is especially true if our strong convictions are matched with a lack of humility and we look arrogantly down on other parents who hold different convictions. It tears apart relationships. Legalism is born when we judge others by our personal standards. This type of attitude has to be extinguished if a long-term relationship is going to be established.

Engaging with an organization like the school district will force you to make wise decisions. You will have to decide which battles are worth fighting and when to fight those battles. There is no magic formula to walking those lines, but the lines must nevertheless be walked.

Each district has its own way of doing things. Yet they will all use similar language. People may have similar positions and titles, even if they mean different things in each district. For instance, the superintendent of one district could have an entirely different job description than that of another. School principals will all have the same title, but their role and influence over what happens at their school will vary greatly from district to district.

Some school districts will have very centralized ways of doing things, while others are very much decentralized. For instance, it is very common for schools to be available for rent by sports leagues or organizations such as churches. However, in the district where we are working, the principals have zero say in who uses the campus. In order to rent a facility in our district, you have to go through one department at the district level. In fact, we learned that there is one individual person at the district level who handles all of the scheduling for all sixteen schools. In other districts, this role is decentralized, and each school manages its own campus usage.

It probably goes without saying, but these types of details make a big difference.

Nothing should be assumed on your end.

You must be a learner, first.

There will be systems and structures put in place that have rhyme and reason. But you cannot assume you understand all of that from the start. There will be vocabulary used, but you shouldn't assume meaning. And if you make assumptions about people based on their title, unmet expectations will create unhealthy wedges in relationships and cause unnecessary frustration. A school official will make decisions that you do not understand or maybe even disagree with. When this happens, walk in wisdom, assuming the posture of a learner rather than a revolutionary leader who has come to save the day. Far too many Christians and churches have chosen the latter approach when they begin, and it inevitably hinders long-term, fruitful relationships for all of us.

For the remainder of this chapter we'll focus on helping you gain a better understanding of how school districts generally work and function. First, we will look at the key influencers at school and district levels. Second, we will consider some practical things we should all keep in mind as we seek to humbly posture ourselves in a way that is most beneficial for long-term relationship building.

WHO ARE THE GATEKEEPERS?

I have spent a considerable amount of time working on college campuses. For nine years I worked with college students, and I spent multiple days on campus each week. These campuses ranged from community colleges to major universities. It took me some time to figure out how each school worked, but I eventually learned to find the right people on campus and developed a strategy for doing ministry on different campuses. (I have written about this in two previous books: *College Ministry 101* and *College Ministry from Scratch*.) When I started getting involved in our local school district, I carried over that general strategy into our ministry at our elementary, middle, and high school campuses. Even though the structure and schedule of life varies from school to school and from district to district, the trick is to find the people who hold the keys. It's a bit of an art, but you have to discover who the true decision makers on a campus are, keeping in mind that they are not always who you might initially guess. Finding these people can take a good amount of time, but it is time well spent.

What do I mean?

Consider the fact that the janitors will typically have keys to just about everything in the school. If a room needs to be opened up for someone, they have the keys to do it. Roles like the janitor are often easily overlooked. But in our experience, having a relationship and a connection with the janitor of a school is where we start. This relationship is *invaluable*. When there is a scheduling conflict, they can help you to change rooms on a whim and get into rooms in advance the night before a big event. Janitors have helped me get into the library when I needed to charge some equipment during off hours. The janitor is an example of a strategic relationship, one that has saved us on a number of occasions. People who hold positions like this are critical on so many practical levels. This is one way in which the one-day *projects* we talked about can help you build longer term fruitful relationships.

What about other people?

Who are some other people we should know about and get to know?

Here are some other examples of people who could be a critical connection point for you, depending on the work and ministry you are looking to do. I will give you the general title used as well as a brief understanding of what they do for their job, but it's up to you to figure out who is best to reach out to in your context.

Community Liaison

This person is best thought of as a human bridge. Community liaisons link organizations with the people they serve. They can do this by providing translation for someone who doesn't speak English, which is why this position is often held by a bilingual individual. People who don't speak English well or at all need help understanding things like enrollment forms and teacher conferences. The people who hold this position know families in need, and many schools look to this person to connect those families with outside organizations that can help them practically—like our church! Additionally, this person will often organize volunteer projects in the community that you can come behind. These projects require recruiting students to participate as well as knowing the needs of a community well. This is the perfect person to try to connect with at the local school level. Elementary schools will often have this position, as will some high schools. They can be paid or volunteer. For whatever reason, middle schools seem to be less likely to have them.

Principals

This leadership role, perhaps surprisingly, is less connected to many of the needs. Of course, some principals are more in tune with the needs of the families attending their school. But keep in mind that they also have to lead teachers, develop policies, lead committees, and create budgets. These added responsibilities require them to focus on many long-term issues. Usually, they are able to make policy changes that affect the trajectory of the school's culture. Consider connecting with principals when initiating a conversation about a program within the school setting. Typically, due to the smaller size of the school and having the most parental involvement of any age-stage schooling, elementary school principals tend to have the most connection with parents and families. Middle school principals tend to be more in tune with the students themselves. (Students this age are really discovering social boundaries so they tend to require the most attention from administration: finding outlets for bored students, helping with students that have a hard time in obedience to rules, etc.) High school principals are usually more administrative by nature because there are far more activities that need to be managed and budgeted, and more people to be overseen. You might say they are more "business" minded. I realize I'm generalizing, but I hope that this framework helps give you a head start on building relationships with these key leaders.

Director of Community Relations

This position is almost always held at a district level. These are the people who are the "marketing executives" of the school system because they promote the district and the needs within schools, usually for the purpose of fundraising and grants. They usually have connections with media teams and access to resources such as video and photography. They also coordinate district-wide mailings and newsletter communications. They typically can connect you with the district resource center and are often the individuals who oversee it or started it in the first place. As the person who gets the grants and oversees the fundraising to meet needs, they are also the one who will make the majority of decisions on how the money is spent. If they don't have the authority to make these decisions alone, they will certainly have the most influence with the committees that do.

Prevention Specialists

Usually found at the local school level, prevention specialists may also be represented at the district level as well. Their roles are usually specialized; some focus on speech, others help students with writing or reading skills or other specific needs. Prevention specialists will usually focus more on the "at-risk" kids and those with special needs. They do everything they can do, but they are *always* in need of more resources. If a local school has a person like this, a good place to start is asking where they need help. Usually, they can come up with a list of volunteer needs, such as tutoring, mentoring, and college prep work. In other words, their unmet needs are usually fantastic inroads for lasting relationships.

School Counselors

School counselors are similar to the previous position, but they focus more on the personal and educational needs of children and are available at every level. There are usually more counselors found at the high school level of education than at other levels. Elementary schools will usually have one counselor whereas a high school might have four or five. If a child is having a tough time emotionally, he or she will almost always see the school counselor. But the counselor's role is not limited to emotional or psychological needs, as most of them help in the educational development of students alongside teachers.

These counselors also are the most understanding of the needs of families. They usually know who the homeless or struggling families are and tend to have the most compassion for the children facing those struggles. They have administrative responsibilities as well, documenting the meetings and interactions with students. They can be highly relational and creative and are great people to get to know. They can't tell you *everything* about everyone in need, but from time to time they can use you as a resource. There are some boundaries that you need to understand when it comes to the law and the separation of church and state, but we'll look at that in chapter 7.

Guidance Counselors

Usually limited to middle and high schools, guidance counselors tend to focus more on the long-term educational trajectory of their students. This might require them to do some work with families, but usually they interact one-on-one with students because, for whatever reason, the family is unable to help them think through and prepare for their future. Almost all high schools have guidance counselors who help students prepare college applications or apply for scholarships or grants. They work with kids who struggle academically or with families that have little or no history in college themselves. Volunteering with a guidance counselor can provide some of the best relational connections, both with students as well as parents. Helping in something as practical as a college application naturally leads to conversations about who the student is, how they will budget, family needs, background, etc.

Site Council Teachers

Just about every school will have a committee called something like "Site Council." This group usually will include the principal or assistant principal, parents (usually a max of two or three), and then a teacher from every grade. This group determines how money is spent at the local school in some specific areas. These areas can vary, usually relating to grant money or school events. This group will also typically speak to policies for the school. For instance, they will help establish school policies in regard to Halloween or Christmas. They will make decisions on what is appropriate language to use, whether or not students should dress up for Halloween, or if the school choir should only sing secular "holiday" songs. This is also an avenue required for schools to consider parental concerns. Being on this council can be a fantastic way to get connected, because it not only provides direct connection with the principal but also some of the most engaged teachers.

I serve on the site council of the school my children attend, a position I was invited to take. The invitation came after four years of working with various folks in the school. The site council is usually a place that needs parental involvement. If you are a parent of a student at a school and can be somewhat flexible one day on a monthly basis, ask about participating in this role.

Front Office Manager

If you want to get connected to someone who knows almost everyone's roles and connections, the front office manager is certainly the person. This person is relationally driven and knows the administration, the teachers, and many of the students. The front office manager will often be the one who schedules appointments with the principal or other high-level leaders at local schools. A good way to begin volunteering in an administrative way is to walk into a school, ask for this person, and then offer your help with anything they see fit. You may be required to undergo a background check, of course. And in some cases, it may be easier to volunteer if you have a child who attends the particular school, but many schools will want help even if that isn't the case.

Passionate People

I realize that this is not a formal role in a school, but I can't leave it off this list. I'm not suggesting that some people are passionate and others are not, but the truth is some people will be passionate about the same things you are passionate about. For instance, you may have a natural connection with the coach of a sport you played or a teacher that focuses on an area you enjoy, such as music or pottery or technology. Finding teachers who share your passion can be a fantastic starting place for getting connected and known around campus.

Knowing some of these key players will hopefully help point you in a direction that is both practical and strategic for your context. But keep in mind that it's not all up to you. Be prayerful and know that God is also already at work. As people desiring to reflect God's love, we must assume that God is already doing things . . . and we are simply joining in.

GOD NEEDS TO SHOW UP

I received an email one day from a man I had never met. He was reaching out to meet with me because he was having some struggles in his life. He had attended our church a couple times, but we had never talked personally. In the email he explained his struggle: he was addicted to heroin.

I agreed to meet with him, not knowing how it would turn out. Often people say they want help, but then they won't actually take steps toward freedom in whatever area they struggle. So we met once, it went really well, and we continued to meet for about four months. Because of the sensitivity of his struggle, I of course kept everything confidential. We would meet in public places where we were able to sit to the side and have some privacy as well.

I didn't tell my assistant and never mentioned the nature of his struggle. It was ongoing. He could still function while using the drugs, even going to work high to avoid getting sick from withdrawal. He had a good job and didn't want to lose it, but he was stuck because he would need a minimum of two weeks off to go through withdrawals and be able to function properly.

In addition to talking about his addiction, I was also working with him on his relationship with his parents. He was hiding all of this from them, even though he was still living at home. He had graduated college but hadn't been able to get his own place for financial reasons. His habit had led him to borrow money and then to lie about how he would use it. Clearly, his world was spiraling out of control. In fact, we finally got to the point where he told his parents about his struggle and let them know that he had been meeting with me. I had no idea who his parents were, but I had learned details about them from what he had shared during our times together.

One day, out of the blue, I got a call from his father. He wanted to meet with me, and I of course agreed. He let me know that he wanted to meet for one reason: to thank me for spending time with his son. But as we talked, I began to realize who this man was. Certain connections clicked into place, and I realized that he was a prominent leader in the school district we were working with. He had heard of our church and all we were doing but, like me, he hadn't connected the dots to figure out I was the person working with his son.

I hadn't met with this young man because of his father's influence. I hadn't even known who his father was. But now, in the eyes of this father, I was a person who could be trusted. And he saw me as a person who cared, someone who put words to action and had helped his son during an extremely difficult time. It was personal. This man later became one of our biggest advocates in the school district. He served as a reference for us on at least a few occasions and even helped open some doors that we could not.

That's just a way of saying, "God showed up in ways I could have never strategized."

And regardless of how we strategize or how hard we work, there are times when that's just what we need him to do. So, strategize and focus on loving people as a reflection of who God is but, most importantly, join me in constantly praying for God to just show up in these kinds of ways. It makes all the difference.

CHAPTER 7

CHURCH AND STATE BALANCING ACT

The phrase "separation of church and state" stirs emotions whenever it comes up in a conversation. Usually there are feelings of anxiety on both sides. Christians are fearful of losing their constitutional right to religious freedom. Government employees—and teachers are among them—are fearful of losing their jobs. Everyone is nervous about blurring the lines and not sure where even to draw the line that separates the state from the church. In a climate of fear, Christians assume that they should be passive and privatize their faith. Many teachers and administrators who work for the state are fearful that they will be accused of religious proselytizing, that it might cost them their job and their reputation.

Without clarity and understanding of these laws, too many decisions are made in fear.

As Christians, we are called to live out our obedience to Christ in every area of life. We should not privatize our faith or hide it in a corner, out of the way. Doing this is a violation of Jesus' life and teachings. Jesus pushed his disciples outward to live out their faith in the world. He was called a "drunkard" and "glutton," not because he drank and ate too much, but because he was always around those who didn't fit in with the religious norms of his day. Jesus described the church as a light on a hill, a community that should be visible to the world (Matthew 5:14).

At the same time, we need to recognize that we live in a pluralistic society, and the schools do not have the right to promote a specific religion or to proselytize on behalf of any religion. This is the most critical point Christians must understand as we seek a relationship with our local school and the people who work and teach there. The dividing line between church and state is not drawn to protect the state from those who wish to live out their faith. But we can never fully separate the role of the government from the religious convictions of citizens. The morality of our culture forms the foundation of our laws and is the basis of our civil and social order. From the Pledge of Allegiance to the national anthem and the solemn oaths taken in a court of law, God is mentioned in honoring ways. Americans believe that our rights are gifts from God, not something the government gives to us. They are inherent and foundational, and the role of the government is limited to protect those God-given rights.

Because God is the source of our rights, we recognize God in a variety of ways in our society. At times, our leaders have verbally proclaimed honor to God and our reliance on him to protect our nation. It's part of the language used, even in government. At the end of his speech on May 2, 2011, when announcing the death of Osama bin Laden, President Barack Obama uttered the following words, "May God bless you. And may God bless the United States of America."

This posture of trust and reliance in God is even celebrated through our national motto, "In God We Trust." This phrase was sanctioned in 1955 by an Act of Congress and is prominently displayed upon every U.S. coin and dollar bill. So in some ways, the government and the church are not as "separate" as we might suppose. There are many ways in which religious beliefs continue to inform our laws, forming the foundation for moral decisions. Yet there continues to be a great deal of confusion concerning the proper exercise of religious beliefs and convictions in the public school. That's what we want to look at more closely in this chapter.

Because our cultural roots are derived from the Judeo-Christian tradition, our educational system has historically acknowledged this. Consider the scheduling of school days on the calendar, for example. School calendars typically revolve around Christian holidays like Christmas and Easter. So the school recognizes that there is a role that religious convictions have in our society and among the students who attend. At the same time, however, schools are viewed as "an arm of the state," and everyone in the public education sector is an employee of the government. Whenever a teacher or an administrator or a coach acts, they act as a representative of the state. This means that they need to balance their own beliefs against the differing beliefs of others while recognizing their role in representing the state. The state must respect the religious rights of all citizens by avoiding the appearance of preferring one religious position or belief over others.

This wasn't *always* the case. At one time, religious beliefs were considered part of the educational curriculum. So creationism—the idea that the world was created by God—was taught as scientific fact rather than religious ideology. The Bible was also used as a text for daily instruction until the U.S. Supreme Court officially banned it for that use in 1963 in the Abington v. Schempp case. In this case the U.S. Supreme Court decided eight to one in favor of Edward Schempp, declaring school-sponsored Bible reading in public schools unconstitutional. However, the court did not say that reading a Bible in school was prohibited. Individual students still had the constitutional right to read their Bible. Rather, this ruling clarified that it was unconstitutional for the public school, as a government institution, to sponsor or advocate for the reading of the Bible as a religious text because in doing so it encouraged a *specific religious viewpoint.*

But that's just the tip of the iceberg.

In the Lemon v. Kurtzman case (1971), the U.S. Supreme Court issued a three-pronged measurement that later became the benchmark for determining whether or not there was a violation of the separation of church and state in public schools. The three measurements were stated in this way:

1. *Schools must do nothing to prohibit or promote religion.* A school should seek to be neutral on matters of religious views, and they can do this by allowing every student to voluntarily choose to participate in activities. As an example, you will often find elementary schools where students participate in alternative activities during the Halloween season. Parents have requested that their child *not* be involved in activities related to the Halloween holiday, and the school must respect that request. Teachers are commissioned to find alternatives for the children who cannot or do not want to participate in dress-up days or other activities related to Halloween. The goal is to make sure every child feels comfortable in the school environment.

Another option a school can pursue is to offer a broad mix of different perspectives, allowing for a variety of religious expressions along with secular, non-religious ones. For example, during the Christmas season choir teachers will often mix a variety of religious songs with secular songs to ensure balance and equal representation and remain within legal boundaries of their job. The goal is the same: they cannot promote or advocate for any one particular religious view.

2. *Schools must be motivated by a secular purpose.* While motives are more difficult to determine, it is important that the stated goal of an activity is non-religious. Again, this is not intended to be discriminatory, barring the practice of a particular religion while allowing others. Rather, it is to help keep the school curriculum focused on core academic subjects like mathematics, history, and language.

3. *Schools must avoid excessive entanglement.* This third point is more difficult to measure and evaluate, so it tends to be fairly subjective. The goal is to ensure that government employees avoid getting "entangled" in the religious activities of their students. This point was clarified in the case of Westside Board of Education v. Mergens (1990) where the U.S. Supreme Court

ruled that students' rights provide freedom for them to exercise their religious beliefs on school grounds, and such activities must be honored by the school. The need to respect student freedom was emphasized here with two clear caveats: (1) the activities cannot cause a "material or substantial disruption" or pose "a clear and present danger" to anyone, and (2) school personnel must avoid entanglement with these groups and, if they attend such activities, they must do so in a "non-participatory capacity."

So what does all that mean? These points have been widely interpreted to mean that the activities should be student led. This is why you will typically find groups or clubs that meet on high school campuses being led by students. While a teacher may be present, they are there in an advisory and supportive role, but they are a "non-participant" in leading the group. This is most often the case with Christian clubs on campus. You will see a teacher there, but they are not there in an official or leadership role. They are supporting the event at the request of the students. Generally speaking, there is some flexibility in this area, but make no mistake . . . there are lines that can't be crossed. If you have questions or doubts about what is appropriate, it's best to sit down and talk with a school administrator at your local school. The way these laws are embraced or enforced can vary.

So these are the broad strokes that guide our involvement. To boil it all down for you: public school employees work for the United States government, and they are hired to provide the community with the core tenants of a good education as defined by the state. As employees of the state, they cannot be expected to support or promote a particular religion. Those activities fall outside the parameters of their job, as well as the legal boundaries set for the school as a public, government-sponsored institution. Of course, this leaves Christian teachers and administrators and counselors in a place of tension. As Christians, they are called to live out their faith in following Jesus, but they must do so within the guidelines set as representatives of the state. Other Christians in their faith community—especially those who have leadership roles in the church—must recognize that these tensions exist and should avoid placing unrealistic expectations on teachers and administrators. There are limits to what they can say and do.

In my own experience, I've found that schools genuinely want to support the religious convictions of the students who attend the school. They recognize that religious beliefs and convictions play a significant role in students' lives. I once had the principal of a local school who is not a believer share in our church services.

As I interviewed him, he talked honestly about how community involvement is needed for the holistic care of students and specifically called out churches as key contributors to the community. He issued a challenge to the people in our church to get involved . . . and, of course, had some ideas for how they could do that!

That said, it is important to note that the specifics of implementing the three-pronged measurement will vary from school to school, from community to community. Some schools will have policies in place already, but some will not. This will vary from school to school and even within the same district. For example, when we started working in our district, we found that some schools had policies about holidays and what a teacher could say or do on those days, while others did not. Keep in mind that the individuals who interpret policies and make decisions will also vary in their personal convictions. Additionally, the policies will depend on the culture of the community and the religious beliefs of the parents in that community. One community might have more Muslim or Jehovah's Witnesses whose children attend, while another might have a large contingent of Catholic or Protestant Christians. Some people within the school will be louder in their complaints. For better or worse, all of these variables will affect the policies a particular school has and how they are implemented.

So what's the takeaway from all of this? *Do not assume anything about your school.* You should walk cautiously as you establish a relationship with the teachers and administrators. Lines may have been drawn in places you don't know about. At the same time, educate yourself before you talk with the school. It never hurts to be aware of the issues and to know the broad boundaries that cannot be crossed. Show that you understand that the employees of public schools cannot advocate religion and they must assume a non-participatory role when a religious activity is happening on campus.

It's that simple. Those who are Christian believers are called to obey the law, to be subject to the governing authorities without resisting them (Romans 13:1–2), and to show honor by being subject to human institutions that are in authority (1 Peter 2:13–17). Parents, teachers, pastors, administrators, and students—we must walk carefully, not putting unfair expectations on the employees of our schools.

We should not pressure school employees to cross legal boundaries simply because they are Christians. Instead, know clearly what the schools can and cannot legally do. Knowing this will help us walk forward together in serving students and the community with confidence. With wisdom and a bit of creativity, we can learn to navigate the legal boundaries with freedom.

THINKING LONG TERM

Recently, I ate lunch with one of the newer principals in our district. It was the first time we had a chance to spend some extended time together one-on-one. I was pleased to learn more about him and immediately was impressed to see how much he cared about the children attending his school. I believe he has the best interests of the students in mind, he cares deeply about the teachers, and he is working very hard to make the environment of the school an even better place for everyone. The school is not perfect, and there are many things that need to be fixed, but he sees the problems, is doing all he can, and is graciously trying to move things forward.

It's encouraging to see.

To my knowledge this man is not a Christian, but I highly respect him and how he is approaching his job. I hope to work closely with him for many years to come, coming behind his vision at the school. That said, I am not shy when I tell people why I want to be involved. I am not a government employee, and so I am clear about my reasons for wanting to serve the school and assist them *in their mission*. In our initial meeting I told him that I am a Christian and how I see serving my school as the best way I can serve my community as a Jesus-follower. As I respected his position and perspective, he respected mine.

We are now at a point where our church is trusted by the school district, so I feel more freedom to have this type of discussion in initial conversations. But, as you can tell from my conversation with the HR director in chapter 1, I have never felt the need to hide my faith. I respect what the teachers and administrators do, and they respect what I do. They understand our Christian motivation as a church. Our motive has never been an issue in engagement. On the other hand, what has caused tension is the history of how Christians before us have approached the school.

Some have approached their local public school as if they are entering enemy territory. Others have approached the school arrogantly, as if they had all the answers to the school's "problems." Still others have offered to help, carrying an assumption that they should be able to share about Jesus openly in the school or have an open prayer station at school-sponsored events with full support of the school. I agree that being able to do those things would be awesome, but demanding them or assuming these are necessary to engage shows our ignorance of the law and forces school employees into an uncomfortable position. It also reveals our shortsightedness with our missional mentality. This attitude lacks humility and is often adversarial. This approach reeks of a desire for power and control rather than giving the aroma of love. We are not to fight against them; we are to serve them as Jesus would.

A shortsighted approach never produces lasting fruit. Trying to force Christian expressions of faith onto the school's agenda only creates a battle that cannot be won. It inevitably results in greater divide between the church and the community. If we want to have an impact, we need to take the long-term approach.

Again, keep in mind that I live in one of the most secular and liberal cities in the United States, and yet I have not once been denied an opportunity to help because my underlying motive was religious in nature. I have always been honest about that. On the contrary, I have been embraced and welcomed. Yes, there have been questions, and some have been afraid of crossing legal lines that separate church and state. But we've been clear about what we are doing and why we are doing it. And this openness, coupled with acknowledging the laws that bind the school's role, has ultimately helped generated trust.

There have been many ways we have built that trust through what we do. Our medical and dental clinics are a good example of this. The school district partnered with us on every level, even funding most of the marketing for the events for our first clinic. The school district's logo was on the flyer next to our church logo. Our church partnered with the school in serving the people of our community for this one-day event. However, some churches declined to participate in the event because they could not openly "preach the gospel." For them, not being able to verbally witness about Jesus was deemed to be a poor use of their time. One pastor was overtly condescending toward me when we discussed this, suggesting that I was not being faithful to Jesus and the gospel by partnering with the school in this way.

I respect the fact that he has a differing opinion on this than mine, but let's consider the options. If "open air preaching" had been allowed I'm sure that someone would have objected that the school was advocating or promoting a religious viewpoint. That would have been a clear violation of the law, and the school principals and district employees would have been in trouble for promoting the event through flyers and calls. So one option is to violate the law, which would have likely put a huge wrench in any partnerships moving forward. Another is to drop the entire program and go back to finding ways to engage the poor without the local school.

I believe there is a third way we can pursue—the way we are discussing in this book.

It is shortsighted to look at the limitations placed on this one-day event and forget that it was giving our church wide exposure within the broader community over the course of the year. Sure, we had to give up control over the one-day event. Compromise is a reality for any relationship or partnership. We were there to serve in whatever capacity the school needed us to serve. But to be clear, in giving up power and control we weren't compromising our own beliefs. We were serving as followers of Jesus, placing the needs of others above our own. And, we had a bigger picture in mind. As I've said, the clinic is not the end goal. It is a means to an end. So, we accepted the fact that we couldn't "preach" to people as they ate their lunch on this one day because there were 364 of days in the year the school district would send people our way.

With this approach, we adopt the posture of Jesus as he served the people in his own community. Jesus never compromised what he believed, and he went out of his way to serve those in need. He did not come to lead a political revolution or fight a war with flesh and blood. He came to serve by giving himself as a sacrifice, leading through his humility and submission to the Father. He trusted that the Father was in control, working out his purposes through Jesus' arrest, suffering, and death. When Jesus "fought," it was to advocate for the poor and the outsiders to have a place where they were welcome at the table. And he did this by focusing his ministry on them and serving them in their need. A simple reading of the four Gospels will show this clearly.

We need to think more deeply about how we can engage with the world around us. Rather than demanding control in order to have an impact, we should seek to have a humble presence of service, trusting God to impact whomever he wishes, however he wants to do it.

In his prayer in John 17, Jesus says that we are not taken out of the world, but remain in it. This means that there is always a need to walk in this tension between the fallen world and our calling to a life of holiness. The balance is found in following the selfless posture and ways of Jesus.

For our part, we must be bold in our actions and with our words, while respecting the position God has given us in our relationship under the laws of our land. In working with the school district, which is bound by certain laws, we use wisdom and take steps with a long-term perspective. Doing our best to relieve the employees of the legal tensions they face is one way we can wisely walk the lines that have been drawn for us. Thankfully, there are several ways to do this.

PROVIDING FREEDOM FOR MINISTRY

Let me say at the outset that people will not believe in Jesus if they have not heard the gospel (Romans 10:14). Followers of Jesus should proclaim how excellent God is through both words (1 Peter 2:9) and deeds (Matthew 5:9–13). In order to do this effectively in our partnership with a public school, some creativity is necessary. Here are three examples that I hope will give you a sense of how you can actively participate in God's mission of reconciling the world to himself through

Jesus (2 Corinthians 5:14–19) and doing so in a way that employees of the school can support.

Partnering with Schools

Fowler is a middle school in our area where we identified several practical needs with some at-risk kids. I spoke with the principal and offered to send an employee to the school on a full-time basis to help them. The needs of the neighborhood were simply too vast for the meager resources they had available. They needed help and they knew they needed help, but the principal wasn't sure about my suggestion. She felt that having a Colossae Church employee working for them was a bit too close to the legal line separating church and state. So we tried to get creative and come up with a solution. How could we help the school meet their needs in a way that would not compromise the law, helping the principal feel not only comfortable but excited about our church serving her school?

I described this briefly before, but after looking at a few ideas, we finally decided to create a job description through the AmeriCorps program. I met with the principal to develop a job description that best fit the needs of the school, we sent in our application to AmeriCorps, and the job was ultimately approved. Having an AmeriCorps–approved job meant that we could meet the need as a church in a way that respected the legal tensions the school employees face on a daily basis. The principal obviously knew that we (as a church) had developed and funded the position, yet the employee was also responsible directly to the AmeriCorps program. We were able to choose the employee for AmeriCorps, so we chose an individual (Michael) from our church to hire for the position. Thinking outside the box like this allowed us to show the principal that we respected her limitations while still providing a much-needed resource for the students and the school. She was able to publicly introduce Michael as an AmeriCorps member who was there to help, but when appropriate share how our church funded the position.

But that is a formal program we developed. Any individual, and especially parents, can simply offer themselves as a resource. Nobody is checking religious identity cards at the front doors of schools! There is simply a need for safe people from the community to help. More of us should take advantage of simply being a "member of the community who cares."

Working with a Homeless Student

In chapter 4, I shared that the greatest need in our area has been providing help for homeless students. Our homeless shelters are underrepresented and overstretched, booked up for months and months. The gentrification of the urban core of Portland has pushed the poverty out deeper and deeper into the suburban areas of Portland. School counselors are constantly dealing with students who have nowhere to live: those who are couch surfing, living in a car, or staying temporarily in a motel. These students are often struggling in school because of inconsistency in their family life. And these families face the real possibility that the state will step in and take their children from them (as biological parents struggling to fight poverty). Counselors are faced with a difficult situation. They want to meet the needs of the families, but if they refer students *exclusively* to a church they run the risk of this being perceived as violating the law. Our church takes many calls from counselors, and while some are grateful that we can help, others are nervous and fearful when they first call us. To help alleviate some of the fears in working directly with a church, we have partnered with an organization called Safe Families. Safe Families is a nonprofit organization staffed by people who attend our church. It is not technically a ministry of our church but a separate and distinct nonprofit. This distinction allows the school counselors to refer families to us through an outside organization, so no laws are violated. The families in need are referred to Christian families who attend our church or another local church in our area.

If you are interested in more details about this program, I've laid out some specifics in Appendix A. If you have a Safe Families ministry near you, it could be a good way for you to engage a school. Many of their connections with families in crisis come through a relationship with schools! This could be a simple way for you to engage immediately in meaningful ways through hospitality.

Working through the "Back Door"

Although the church as a religious organization needs to be a bit more creative in how we approach schools, at the core good works that are implemented should be universally received. Any organization, religious or not, desiring to do good in a school should be welcomed. The outreach to the community by Christians or churches does not constitute a violation of church and state separation. We cannot separate our faith from what we do, but it is possible for us to do things without inappropriately forcing our religious beliefs on others. We build trust and relationships through helping others, demonstrating what we believe. And our love for and relationships with people will cause us to articulate our message carefully.

I've already mentioned our medical and dental clinics and how they have met a huge need with the underinsured of our area. And we have offered this help in intimate partnership with our local school district. For the most part, we are very open about our faith. The majority of our volunteers are Christian. In fact, the last clinic we did we had over forty-eight churches represented.

However, there are times when we are not initially verbal with our beliefs, having to highlight our witness to Jesus through the "back door." When our guests come to be served, we sit down with each of them and find out if there are any other needs they have that would not be met in the one-day clinic. We take note of these needs and every guest is asked if they would like a "volunteer from this clinic to contact them afterward to follow up with them in a relational way to discuss these." The majority of guests say they would like that. This means that there are Christians who follow up with these individuals *outside of the event*. This provides volunteers with a natural way of getting to know the guests who attend and ask for help, perhaps praying with them or inviting them to church in addition to helping with their practical needs. This sort of creativity walks the separation of church and state lines well.

These things increase our presence in the community. Not everyone can provide full-time employees to the school district like our church does, but we can all participate as followers of Jesus. Sure, it requires some knowledge of the basic laws and perhaps some creativity, but most of all it just requires a willingness to pay the price of time and to show up. In this simple way we can freely be who we are: people who love, enjoy, and proclaim Jesus to the world around us through everything we do and say. And nobody has a problem with it.

CHAPTER 8

UNDERSTANDING CONTEXTS

"Location, location, location."

That's the phrase that comes up whenever someone is talking about real estate. The underlying assumption is the value of your home will largely be determined by where it is located. It's very true.

I was recently in Sunnyvale, California, staying at my wife's parents' home. We were there doing some day trips all around the Bay Area. One day we went to San Francisco, another to Santa Cruz, another to an amusement park. One afternoon we saw a sign for an open house that was only a few blocks from where we were staying. We stopped by to tour.

My wife and I stop by open houses frequently. It's sort of a fun little thing we do as a family. We see a sign and, if we have time, stop in to see the place. I love looking around because it gets me out of my routine, and I find myself envisioning what I would do with the house, which walls I would take out, what updates I would make. It's just a little thing my wife and I enjoy doing . . . and then we leave.

This particular home was just under 1,800 square feet, three bedrooms and two baths. It had a good-sized front yard, but the backyard was small. It was a mid-century home that had a few updates but was mostly out-of-style, though some original features gave the home a unique character. We aren't fans of cookie-cutter homes, so we liked that. On the West Coast, these mid-century homes are often bought by younger families and redone with a more modern feel, with a minimalist decor of raised ceilings and concrete floors.

So the home was clean—but not that nice—and the sale price was $1.4 million solely because of its location. That same home would have sold for far, far less anywhere else in the United States. But it was located near Facebook, Apple, and Google, and the location shot up the price. That price point limits who the potential buyers will be. We wondered, "Who could possibly afford to buy this home?" Well, apparently many people. The house sold in just two days.

Location matters.

Where you live matters. There are different community norms and varying socioeconomic statuses from community to community, city to city. In this final chapter, I'd like to walk you through a brief overview of locations. These are contexts that differ greatly and yet have one thing in common: the school district is the key to embrace the biblical mandate of love through the gospel toward the poor and disadvantaged in that community.

I believe these three contexts represent some of the diversity of North American culture: urban core, suburban, and rural. As you read about each context, take note of the differences and the similarities. Where you live may match one of these, or it may be a mix of two of them. Differentiating where you live from these descriptions will really help you in understanding the nuances that might just give you a head start when you initiate with your school. Your location will affect what you do and how you go about it.

C. S. Lewis once said: "Show me a man that is well traveled and I will show you a man that knows the lies of his own village." His point is that the more we learn about other places and cultures, the better we are able to see our own culture with fresh perspective. By becoming a student of the ways and thinking of others, we learn to see our own world through a different lens. Remember, the mission field is not *everywhere* other than where you live. Your location is a mission field, and thinking about where you live in relationship to other contexts is a key step toward you showing love by serving your local school.

Context One: The Urban Core

Urban communities tend to revolve around the center of a city, and they are often made up of unique cultural areas. There is often an "old city" with historical buildings or architecture. There may be some "new city" aspects such as skyscrapers, offices, and apartment-style housing. There may be a business district, a shopping district, and various ethnic communities. Urban communities, in general, have higher costs of living, higher pollution, and there is generally a much faster pace to life. There are frequently diverse transportation options and neighborhoods filled with coffee shops, grocery stores, and restaurants. While people have cars, they are far less necessary than they are in rural or suburban contexts.

Many urban communities are facing the challenge of gentrification. Gentrification is defined as the process of renewal and rebuilding of deteriorating areas that often displaces poorer residents with an influx of middle-class or affluent people. In other words, it's taking the run-down areas of an urban core and making them nicer. This increases the cost of living of an area, which inevitably displaces the poorer people that once lived there. This is why gentrification is called "yuppification" by some critics. Yuppification refers to the catering of yuppie tastes like sushi and Starbucks. It's not just residents that are moved out but businesses as well. Older businesses are essentially run out of the neighborhood because of the rapid rise of rental rates in the area.

In Portland, where I live now, there have been several gentrification projects over the past twenty years. An area called "The Pearl District"—what was once a community of rundown warehouses, abandoned buildings, and lower-income housing—is now one of the most affluent areas of our downtown area. This sort of urban development changes both the appearance and the social fabric of these areas. City officials speak of this gentrification process as "urban renewal," but those in the black community sometimes refer to it as "racial removal." This is especially true in northeast Portland. Much of this area was once the home of the black community, but many of them were pushed out by gentrification. One potential positive in this is some of the churches in this area are growing in ethnic and cultural diversity because residents of higher socioeconomic statuses are moving into the area. However, one of the downsides is many in the black community have been pushed further east and now commute in to attend their church.

In many urban communities today, the poor are actually being pushed out of the urban core and into more suburban contexts, where there are far less resources like rescue missions and food pantries. Yet those living in suburban contexts still seem to think primarily of the urban core when they think of poverty. It is important to wrap our minds around the cultural shift gentrification creates—especially for those living in a suburban context.

CONTEXT TWO: SUBURBAN CONTEXTS

Suburbs are those communities formed on the fringes of the city. They are usually nestled between the business of city life and the peace of the rural areas. Families can enjoy both extremes within a short drive. Suburbanites experience the same type of community organizations found in the city (hospitals, police, etc.). Some suburbs may have some sort of "downtown" area, but they typically center around shopping centers and schools. Housing is usually less expensive than in the city, but this can vary.

As mentioned earlier, in many regions of the U.S. the poor are beginning to settle more in suburban contexts. In fact, as Katie Rose Quandt responds to the rise of poverty in an article for the *New York Times* she writes: "But the location of the struggling households within these metro areas goes against our ingrained notions about poverty and the inner-city. So far this century, more than two-thirds of the poverty increase occurred in households located in the suburbs, not the cities proper."[4] In many locations those in the suburbs are not well equipped to deal with rapidly rising poverty rates. As Elizabeth Kneebone, coauthor of a Brookings Institution report, told *The Atlantic*, "Many of these communities lack the infrastructure, safety-net supports, and resources to address the needs of a growing poor population, which can make it that much harder for poor residents to connect to the kinds of opportunities that can help them get out of poverty in the long run."[5] The suburbs typically have less access to public transit and fewer social services than are found within the cities they surround.

The challenge of suburban poverty is not immediately visible to us. Most drive right past the needs of the poor in these communities. Many in the suburbs are struggling to navigate job changes or losses. They find themselves in a position of having to choose between paying the phone bill or putting gas in their car.[6] Many families find themselves in positions of need, yet they continue to live in the same home, dress in the same clothes, and drive the same car. Therefore, families with higher needs can often go unnoticed and unseen. To fill the gap, many public schools are trying their best to meet the needs of these families through social services and school district–run resource centers. However, the need is far greater than what they can handle.

That is, unless Christian individuals and churches are connected with the local school.

As Christians, we should be aware of where we live and the surrounding circumstances that affect it. The tensions of our neighborhoods and communities should matter to us. God has placed us where we live because he wants to use us where we live, and frankly, if we don't think God wants to use us to express his love toward the poor and disadvantaged where we live . . . well then, we need to move. If you live in a suburban context and don't think there are needs to be met where you live . . . just get involved with the school district.

CONTEXT THREE: RURAL AREAS

Living the rural life is very different from life in either an urban or suburban setting. Family life may be centered around livestock or agriculture. There is often a more communal culture, and community organizations, such as the police, hospitals, fire departments, and schools, are all a key part. Sometimes, due to limited financial resources, these services are spread out between multiple communities.

Rural America is uniquely diverse. No single industry dominates the rural economy across the United States, no single pattern of population decline or growth exists for all rural areas, and no statement about improvements and gaps in the well-being of people (i.e., poverty or wealth) holds true for all in rural contexts. Each region is different. Logging and sawmills are largely found in the Pacific Northwest and New England, manufacturing in the Southeast and Midwest, and farming in the Great Plains. These types of differences cause the needs of an area to vary greatly.

Poverty takes on different forms depending on the state of the economy and of the particular industry that dominates in an area. Among rural areas, census data tells us that poverty is concentrated more heavily in the southeastern United States. Poverty means that there may be less access to advanced telecommunications services, limited availability of natural resources, and possibly farther distance from a major metropolitan area. Other variances in poverty are affected by the amount of transportation and shipping facilities, the political history and structure, and the racial, ethnic, and cultural makeup of the population.[7]

In other words, there are a lot of factors to think about. Following Census Bureau recommendations, we now use the American Community Survey (ACS) when we are looking for national poverty statistics. This ACS metric began in 2009 and now serves as the national standard for determining poverty levels. Poverty thresholds were developed in the 1960s and are adjusted annually to account for inflation. They represent the federal government's estimate of the point below which a family of a given size has insufficient cash income to meet basic needs. Any family/individual with total income less than an amount deemed to be sufficient to purchase food, shelter, clothing, and other essential goods and services is classified as poor.[8]

The amount of income necessary to purchase these basic needs is set by the Office of Management and Budget (OMB). Poverty thresholds are set for families by size and composition, and they are updated annually to correct for inflation.[9]

Keep in mind that U.S. poverty rates do not adjust for differences in cost of living in comparison to other contexts. So while these reports give us a general picture of poverty in an area, the actual level of well-being experienced by people in one context can be overstated or understated depending on the cost-of-living index. This is why being involved in a local school helps you. Through this relationship, you will grow in your understanding of the actual context around you.

EXEGETING YOUR CONTEXT

The word *exegesis* literally means "a critical interpretation." It has the idea of drawing out meaning so that we can apply it practically to our lives. This idea can be applied to where you live. For you, this should be considered the primary context where God is at work today. Through careful, sensitive, and critical (discerning) observation, your task is to discover the truth of God's presence and activity where you live and then respond practically to that activity. God wants to use us where we live. I say this with one caveat: rather than looking to your community to find its problems, I would first highly recommend trying to find strengths and looking for places where God is already at work where you live.

There are most certainly things to celebrate, and one of the most common mistakes people and especially church leaders make is that they don't first understand how God is *already at work*. So we go into a place thinking we are going to change the world by bringing something nobody else is doing. It's a weird posture of power rather than service, and it is damaging. There are faithful people where you live who are doing amazing things. Find these people and first celebrate what God is already doing through them in your local school.

This will help you in a number of ways. First, it will help you eventually see the needs that are not currently being met. But second, and perhaps even more importantly, you will posture yourself as a true servant. By coming in and first celebrating what is already happening, you build unity and trust with the others whom you will be working alongside.

In addition to this humble approach, you can take

some time and steps forward personally or with a small group of people. There are some very practical things I would recommend doing after you finish this book that are simple but can really help you articulate where you live much better. Each of us can stand to learn more about where we live, all of which will help you as you interact with the schools in your community. If you're really bold or in a ministry position, you may even ask to meet with administrators at your local school and ask them some of the questions I will list below. They will likely have answers to many of them simply because they are faced with the tensions every day. Learn as much as you can from as many people as possible.

Where you live deserves your attention and focus, and the time you give to understanding where you live is the extent to which you can be a faithful presence. As we conclude the book, I'd like to leave you with some practical ideas for better understanding the location where God has currently placed you:

1. *Walk around neighborhoods.* Start with your own, of course. It's one thing to drive streets and another to walk them. Walking or biking around helps us gain a more informed perspective on an area.

2. *Draw a map of your area.* The map can be general, but include where your home is, the

basic street patterns, where your church is, where schools are, any major landmarks, core shopping areas, parks, etc.

3. *Grab a notebook and pen.* Then go for another walk, stopping in shops and certainly a coffee shop where you can grab a cup of coffee. Notice the architecture, types of trees, types of cars, or people. Write down anything that stands out to you.

4. *Research your city.* Do a simple Google search on your city/town to get some census information. Note the history of where you live. What key people have lived there? Were there critical turning points in the life of the city you live in?

5. *Take note of the key gatekeepers for your city.* What major corporations, organizations, or people have impact on the economic status of the community or are major influencers in general? What industries are prominent?

6. *Get personal.* What people groups are in your neighborhood? Is there ethnic diversity? If so, which are the geographical areas of your city where specific ethnic groups tend to settle?

7. *Get economic.* What is the median household income of where you live? What evidence of struggle, poverty, despair, or neglect do you see? Is your community stable, growing, or dying?

8. *Understand public areas.* What public spaces are provided for children, teenagers, or seniors? Are they being used? If so, in what ways? Is there a local park? What do you notice about it? Does it feel like an inviting place? Who is there? How is it used?

9. *Evaluate your context.* What words or phrases best describe your neighborhood?

10. *Consider potential partners.* What are some ways churches are already engaging the core of your context? What other parachurch or nonprofits are in your area? What are they doing? Who are they reaching? Who are the influential leaders in them?

11. *Evaluate transportation and safety.* Imagine yourself as an older person with no car or as a young child living in the middle of this neighborhood. How disadvantaged or advantaged would you be with respect to shops, churches, parks, or schools? Are there places in your neighborhood that you wouldn't go? Why?

12. *Identify the positive.* Where are the places of life, hope, beauty, or community?

13. *Look for the Spirit.* In what ways do you sense God's presence where you live?

The final question leads me to offer one last suggestion for you before you get to work. In most cases, there are programs already happening at your local school, programs that may need additional help or volunteers. The simplest way to start is by joining an existing team. Educate yourself and find out if there are other organizations already at work at the school. There are national organizations that are relationally centered, and you can easily find more information about them online, including groups like Young Life or Student Venture or Big Brothers Big Sisters or The Mentoring Project. If you loved athletics when you were in school, consider joining the Fellowship of Christian Athletes chapter in your area. If you love prayer, you can find out who is in charge of the annual See You at the Pole event and start there. These are great opportunities to dip your toe in the water, meet people, and see where things might lead from there.

I want to leave you with two final questions and then one last challenge. If you are someone who claims to be a follower of Jesus . . . what are you doing to reflect his love to those around you? How are you serving the disadvantaged and the poor where you live? If you don't have a good answer to those questions, then pray about how God might want to use you to serve in your local school. It's a strategic place to start—regardless of where you live.

If I tell my daughter to go clean her room, the last thing I want her to do is come back to me twenty minutes later and demonstrate that she's memorized what I said to her. And I certainly don't want her to give me a five-minute talk on what it *would* look like to obey her father and creative ways she could do that. I simply want her to do what I ask her to do. To listen to what I say and then put it into action.

How often do we, as followers of Christ, do something with what we read or hear God saying to us besides memorizing it or talking with others about what it *would* look like if we actually did it? I hope you've found this book helpful. But my greater hope is that you won't just find it to be an interesting read with thought-provoking ideas. I pray that you will be different after reading this book because you will actually *do* something . . . rather than just talking about it. That's what God wants from each of us. Let's not just be hearers of the Word—let's do what Jesus says. The difference between those who do something in this world versus those who don't is simple: those who do something actually do something.

Appendices

SAFE FAMILIES

A VISION DOCUMENT

The following is part of the research report that some leaders of Colossae Church prepared before starting and implementing our Safe Families strategy. If you are a church leader, this can give you a framework of understanding as well as implementation of a similar program.

THE PROBLEM: FAMILIES IN CRISIS

How do you define a "crisis"? The term refers to a turning point, a place that is unstable or dangerous. In social and economic affairs, a turn at that moment can lead to a decisive change. It's a point that determines all future events, for better or worse.

Through conversations with the police department and the school district, we've been alerted to the growing number of families who are at a turning point. We face a true crisis regarding homelessness in our community.

To solve this problem, children are often taken from their parents, despite the initiative shown by some parents to find work and a home.

Homelessness is probably not the first problem you think of in our suburban context of Tigard, Tualatin, Beaverton, and Hillsboro. Yet after months of working with the school district's family resource center, we have been astounded by the large numbers of local homeless families and children that are referred to us every week.

A Typical Profile

A couple was recently referred to the Tigard/Tualatin resource center who had an eight-year-old son attending an elementary school. The family was homeless and living in their car, parking every night at a rest stop to sleep. They would take their son to school in the morning, and then spend their day searching for both employment and housing. They were able to get on the county's shelter waiting list but were without options as they waited. Thankfully, a church allowed them to stay inside the building for a short time but could not provide that type of shelter long term for legal/zoning reasons. This left the family with their car as their only option. Unfortunately, due to his inability to shower on a regular basis, the son suffered from an infection. The family obviously struggled to keep food they bought from spoiling without access to a refrigerator. Eventually, a storm caused severe damage to one of the windows in the family's car, and sadly, due to safety concerns, the son was removed from the situation by Child Protective Services.

We've asked: "How can our church help?" The reply from both the school district and the police department is that they need help dealing with the problem of homelessness. That is consistently seen as the number one need in our community. So, after four years of hearing about the need and seeing it firsthand, we have developed a strategy for assisting in this area.

As a church, we have intentionally pursued exposure to the needs in our community through our relationship with the school district. We believe the school district is at the heart of our suburban community, and we have reached out to and served leaders in the school district: employees, counselors, principals, and police officers working on local school campuses. The response from our partners has been overwhelming.

Colossae Church has a full-time employee working at the family resource center to assist the Tigard/Tualatin School District. Unfortunately, when homeless families are referred to the resource center, we have little to offer them to address their housing situation. The current solution is to assist in placing them on a shelter waiting list. Shelters in our area generally have a wait time of at least six weeks, so there are no immediate options available to families. In some cases, families with young children have lived in their car for several weeks waiting for housing to become available. Inevitably, social services gets involved. In some cases, children face the possibility of being taken from the care of their parents, not from lack of care but due to poverty and the lack of housing options. While there are cases where removing the child is best, there are also situations where this is unnecessary. Here is where the church can play a critical role in preventing this family crisis from happening.

First, we need to understand how homelessness is defined by those we are working with. Homeless students are those who lack a "fixed, regular, and adequate nighttime residence." Each school district generally has four categories of students/families that they deem as homeless:[10]

1. *Doubled-Up Families*: These are families who do not have their own home so they may be living with another family, couch surfing with a relative, etc.
2. *Hotel/Motel Families*: These are families who are living in a hotel or motel because they can't afford housing of their own.
3. *Sheltered Families*: These are families currently living in homeless shelters in the area.

4. *Unsheltered Families*: These are families living in extremely substandard dwellings such as cars, parks, RVs, camping sites, etc.

Since the statistics for the 2014–2015 school year were not yet available, we looked at the 2013–2014 school year to obtain data. Below are the numbers that have been reported through school counselors in the fourteen schools that alone make up Tigard/Tualatin:

Homeless Nighttime Living Condition:

Doubled-Up Count	120
Hotel/Motel Count	15
Sheltered Count	29
Unsheltered Count	4
Year End Homeless Count Total:	**168**

In Washington County as a whole, this problem increases.[11]

Every school district keeps a running count throughout the school year of the number of students at each school who are classified as Title IX. This data gets updated on a regular basis and is cumulative throughout the school year.

Tigard School District Homeless Children and Youth for the 2013–2014 School Year

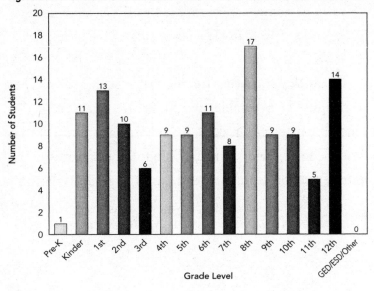

Beaverton School District Homeless Children and Youth for the 2013–2014 School Year

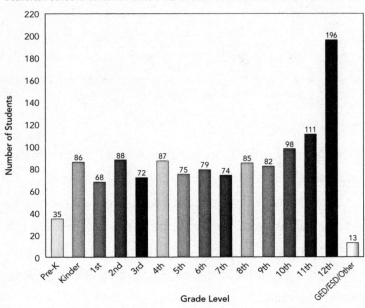

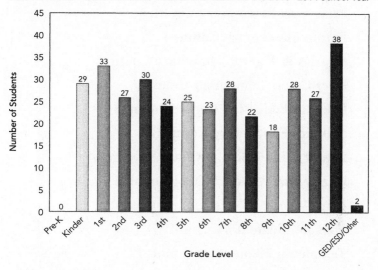

Hilsboro School District Homeless Children and Youth for the 2013–2014 School Year

Homelessness Statistics for the 2014–2015 School Year

Colossae is located in Tigard (directly serving Tigard/ Tualatin School District) and will also be launching another location in Hillsboro in February 2015.

Hillsboro School District (35 schools): As of October 13, 2014, there are 163 students on record as being homeless.

Tigard Tualatin School District (14 schools): As of October 13, 2014, there are 64 students on record as being homeless.

Because we are set to start working in Tigard immediately, here is the current breakdown of the homeless kids in each of the fourteen schools:

Alberta Rider Elementary Count: 1

Bridgeport Elementary Count: 4

Byrom Elementary Count: 3

Charles F. Tigard Elementary Count: 5

Deer Creek Elementary Count: 1

Durham Education Center Count: 4

Durham Elementary Count: 3

Fowler Middle School Count: 6

Hazelbrook Middle School Count: 5

Mary Woodward Elementary Count: 1

Metzger Elementary Count: 6

Templeton Elementary Count: 1

Tigard High School Count: 12

Tualatin Elementary Count: 3

Tualatin High School Count: 5

Twality Middle School Count: 4

Note: As of November 26, 2014, The Tigard/Tualatin School District had an intake of 94 students classified as homeless with 74 students still active in the district, and 20 students no longer enrolled. These figures change daily, and are calculated and recorded on a monthly basis.

The number of homeless students and families in Washington County is on the rise every year. The following chart shows the number of homeless students in the Tigard/Tualatin School District over three consecutive years.

SCHOOL YEAR	NUMBER OF STUDENTS
2010–2011	105
2011–2012	128
2012–2013	202

COMMUNICATING THE GOSPEL

As we approach this expression of mission, we need to understand that there are windows of redemption and opposition to the gospel. Those we are trying to reach have specific geographic boundaries, cultural values, and worldviews that compete with the gospel. Here is a very brief overview of how we understand the importance of each of these:

Geographic Boundaries

Those we are trying to serve are often limited by transportation and are therefore transient in nature. This may seem contradictory at first, but it's a necessity for survival. There is a need to continue moving from place to place. Some are confined to a car and therefore need to find new places to park overnight. Others are going from friend to friend, having to continuously find new sleeping arrangements.

The specific geographical boundaries for our ministry

are within Washington County. In addition we are limiting our service to those connected to our school district. This provides a somewhat different geographical boundary because individual schools have geographical limitations. We chose the school district as the geographic boundary because we want to do our best to keep children in the same school. So we need a geographic strategy based around the location of individual schools.

Cultural Values

Among those we are seeking to serve, survival is a primary cultural value. When people are in a time of crisis, they tend to neglect long-term goals and plans and simply want to push through this stage of life. While this is a normal way to cope with crisis circumstances, it does not lead to long-term solutions. The welfare of the family is sometimes neglected as families try to survive another day, getting their children to another day of school, and in some cases trying to figure out how to get the next meal. As believers we want to offer ourselves to help with their needs, but we need to think long-term, even as we address their short-term needs.

Competing Worldviews

Every person we meet has some views that oppose the gospel. One area where we frequently encounter questions and confusion is in discerning God's presence. God's presence is most commonly evaluated based on how circumstances affect our lives. If things are going well, the conclusion is drawn that God is present and available. However, when things are not moving favorably, doubt of his presence and availability takes over. In fact, it's when things are especially difficult that God is most often questioned and doubted. These families are in crisis, and it should be expected that they are left wondering whether or not God is for them.

We feel like it is our job to communicate the gospel with these issues in mind. Following are a few thoughts on how we can move forward effectively.

Our Posture—Cultural Humility

The goal is to communicate the gospel as accurately as possible. If communication is mostly nonverbal, our approach in serving others has to be considered carefully. Here are a few brief thoughts on how Jesus approached serving others that we might consider.

He Gave Himself

Jesus certainly gave himself in death, but he also gave of himself in life. We don't have any evidence that he just gave money to people, and he was always on the move during his three years of intensive ministry.

However, as he encountered people, we see him extending himself to each individual. In Western culture it is all too easy to just meet a need and then go back to our lives. Generosity can include giving of finances, but the generosity of Jesus was seen most in the giving of himself.

Generosity Was a Means of Service, Not Power

When Jesus served people, it was clear that he put them and their needs above his own. For example, this is seen in the washing of feet. It's an act of humility that instills value in the person. Unfortunately, in Western culture we can often think of ourselves as better than those who have less. We must intentionally process how we are viewing those we are serving so that we can assume the attitude and posture of Jesus.

Jesus Saw People, Not Just Needs

It wasn't always the case, but Jesus often told those he healed to not tell anyone what had happened. Some of this may have been due to the distraction of crowds, but as one reads these encounters, it is obvious Jesus is meeting the person through the needs. We must be cautious of meeting needs as a means to convert people. Instead, our desire to communicate the gospel is realized in meeting people where they are . . . and part of that is meeting the needs.

Opportunities to Communicate the Gospel

The gospel is most accurately communicated by a community of people who believe it and live by it.[12] Our individual efforts of proclamation only gain credibility when it flows out of a local, worshiping community. A community of people who understand their salvation will be devoted to good works (Titus 2:11–3:8). A community that proclaims God's reign lovingly through language and works is a community that is going to actively join in God's mission of reconciling the world to himself through Jesus (2 Corinthians 5:14–21).

A COMMUNITY-BASED STRATEGY

We believe Christian community is a means for benefiting others (Hebrews 10:23–25).

We believe the gospel is best communicated in the context of a local, worshiping community.

We therefore have developed a community-based approach to serving families in crisis, but this doesn't come without obstacles. We see at least three obstacles we need to overcome in this expression of mission:

1. *Personal burnout.* Continuously giving of self becomes burdensome without community or

boundaries. Our model therefore provides unique roles that individuals assume as part of a larger community, which provides boundaries of protection.

2. *Separation of church and state.* The sad reality is employees within the school district have fairly strict limitations on the resources they can point people in need to. They are able to mention Colossae Church, but (1) they cannot solely recommend a church, and (2) if they do mention a local church as a resource, they must also recommend at least two other options. To work through this issue, Colossae has decided to strategically partner with Safe Families for Children, a separate 501(c)3 nonprofit organization that supports local churches in this very issue. Safe Families is a Christian organization completely dependent on the local church to do what it does. However, they are also a legal entity and, therefore, have an easier time being in direct relationship with the school district. They will provide the safe middleman platform for school counselors who know of needs and want to see them met immediately. Counselors will be able to send families in crisis directly to Safe Families for Children without any hesitation. Safe Families

will do the proper legal work ahead of time and then hand off the relationship to the Colossae community.

3. *Legal limitations.* One of the main obstacles in attempting to host families and children who are in crisis, and specifically trying to avoid or overcome homelessness, is the legal liability for both families involved. Our partnership with Safe Families for Children also solves this tension. Safe Families partners with the church to take on the liability of housing underage children. They provide the training for host families within the church. These trainings can either be done online or in the form of a one-day, in-person training with Safe Families representatives. Safe Families also facilitates the screening and approval of both volunteers and families referred to the program through background checks, fingerprinting, home studies, references, interviews, etc.

The Model

Our desire for this expression of mission to be fleshed out through community is matched and supported by the current Safe Families model. The shared desire is for communities within the church to come around a family in crisis, providing housing for the children, and support, prayer, and encouragement as the family tries to get back on their feet. This model is focused on building a *relationship* with children and/or families who often times have very few other caring relationships in their lives.

This is a shared effort where several individuals will assume specific roles in the support of one family in crisis. These roles include:

A Host Family

Host families are volunteer families who are willing to open their homes to children in crisis and provide a safe and loving home and family atmosphere for them on a temporary basis. Host families may choose to host the parents of the children as well, but this is done at their discretion and is not the regular model. However in some situations (i.e., young single moms) it is best to keep the parent with the child in the placement. Host families will go through a screening process led by Safe Families for Children. They can specify what age of child/type of family they would like to have placed with them. When Safe Families receives a referral for a family that seems to be a match, they will contact the host family and set up a meeting. Children will not be placed with a host family without the host family's approval, and a hosting situation will end upon the hosting family's request if the placement is not working.

A Respite Family

Respite families are families that partner with a host family to provide temporary (less than one day) care for children to allow the host family to run errands, shop, or simply get a break.

Family Friends

These are volunteers willing to serve in a mentoring role to connect with the biological families of the children being hosted. These volunteers are not professionals but come alongside families in a nonthreatening, non-intimidating manner to offer advice, support, and resources to help the family get back on their feet. The role of a family friend can look different according to the situation. Family friends can offer support to the biological family through prayer, assistance with job applications and interviews, job connections, housing applications, etc.

Prayer Team

This is a family or group of volunteers that commit to pray for the biological and volunteer families on a regular and ongoing basis. The prayer team can also serve as a support group to both biological and volunteer families, facilitating events such as play groups, coffee talks, burger nights, etc.

Resource Family

These are volunteers who commit to helping provide resources for the biological and host family. Most children who will be hosted have very few supplies and possessions. Host families will not be reimbursed for any expense they incur, so it is important to have volunteers willing to donate items such as diapers, formula, cribs, car seats, strollers, etc., to help support host families.

The roles listed above are ideas and examples that have worked well in previous situations, but are not meant to be an exact model for every church.

INTEGRATION OF THE MODEL— AN OVERVIEW

We see this model fitting very well with Colossae's current structuring of community. Rather than one family "adopting" a homeless family or family in crisis, an entire community group will adopt a family. One family within the community would act as the host family, while other members/families within the group will act in one of the roles listed above.

This model is also unique in that the church really creates their own vision and specific model with which to support and house families. This flexible model is critical for collaboration with other churches. Safe Families serves as the legal entity to take on liability, refer families, train, and screen those involved, but each local church and its members will determine what it looks like specifically for them. No two hosting situations are alike. Members of the church determine what demographic of children they are willing/able to take in and what their involvement with the biological family will be. They also determine exactly what role those supporting the host family will play.

The first step for families desiring to be part of this expression of mission is to fill out a survey detailing what they would like their involvement to be. Families interested in hosting will include information regarding what demographic of child/family they would like to have placed with them. This information will be put into a database that will be referenced by Safe Families for Children when attempting to match biological and host families.

Every hosting situation is unique because every family situation and need is unique. Families may host for as little as a few days and for as long as a year, although *the average hosting duration is about six weeks.*

Referrals—"The Process"

Families are referred to the program for a variety of reasons. For example, a pregnant single mother with a few children may have to go to the hospital and have nowhere safe for her children to stay while she is in delivery. Or, children may need a safe home because they are living in their car while their parents look for work. However, with every host situation, the goal is always to build positive caring relationships with children and families in need.

Children will be referred to our network of safe families in a variety of ways. Most often, referrals will come from officials directly tied to the school district such as teachers, counselors, employees of the family resource center, etc., as they are most intimately connected to the people in crisis. Families may also be referred through the local police department or social services. These officials will call the Safe Families coordinator with information about a family they believe would benefit from the program. The state coordinator will then meet with and interview the family, determine if they are a fit for the program, and get details regarding their situation. The coordinator will then search the database of hosts to try to find a likely match. The coordinator will finally contact the host family directly.

Police, School → Safe Families → Church/Host &
District Employee   Coordinator   Community

Staffing Support

Even though Safe Families for Children recommends this ministry be supported by at least one key individual in the local church, Colossae will support this with two staff members who work closely with one another, but each will support distinct areas:

1. *The relationship between schools and Safe Families for Children.* This community liaison role mainly helps coordinate interactions between counselors and Safe Families. Although part of this role is helping those within the church, the main focus is meeting with counselors and other district employees to cast the vision, help answer questions, serve as a resource, and evaluate how each placement is going from all sides.

2. *The communities that participate in this expression of mission.* This is a pastoral role, providing support to the communities that engage in this mission. Although part of this may include dialogue with Safe Families for Children and civic leaders, this role is focused on people *within the church.* The focus is to cast

vision within the church, recruit potential host families, as well as provide practical support and spiritual advice to the communities who are already engaged. There is also no question that we will have to reach outside of Colossae to meet the existing needs, so this staff member will also seek involvement from other churches as well.

The two staff members will work together to coordinate the initial meeting between the host family and biological family. This meeting is vital for the host family to determine whether or not it would be a good idea to move ahead with the placement. If the host family decides to move forward, this will serve as the hand-off point between the two staff members.

COLOSSAE'S ROLE—THE BIGGER PICTURE

Our role is a preventive one, to keep families from being split apart and to provide support through the rebuilding process. Practically, this includes promoting this model and Safe Families for Children as an organization to the larger community, starting with officials in the school district, police officers, and social workers. Our hope is that our partnership with Safe Families for Children will become such a success that we will be the first place anyone thinks of to refer a family in crisis.

We know that addressing this issue is beyond the capacity of any one local church. However, our hope is to champion this model to the larger community as a whole. Our hope is that other churches and members of the faith community, having seen the success that the model can have, might join in and reproduce this model in their own churches and districts. This has in fact been the case in the Chicago area.[13]

Our role as hosting and supporting families will be to provide a safe and caring place for children to be while their parents work to come out of some sort of crisis situation. Throughout this process, however, parents maintain full custody of their children. Our role as a church is to keep children out of the state foster care system and keep families together. Therefore, the families being referred to the Safe Families network will be those who would benefit from a safe and stable environment but also would benefit most from being able to stay with their biological families in the long run.

STRATEGY FOR IMPLEMENTATION WITHIN A CHURCH

There is a process to implementing this model. We officially started our ministry in February 2015 and then formally evaluated in June and December of the same year. Following is an overview of our general timeline for empowering people in this ministry:

November/December 2014: Articulate a written document that explains the problem, solution, processes, and evaluative tools (i.e., this document).

January 2015: Begin meeting with school and city officials, letting them know about our efforts, timeline, and processes. Begin championing the Safe Families for Children model and explain how we will utilize and adapt that blueprint as our foundation. Teach the first three messages of a five-part sermon series, using the current Hebrews series as a catalyst. Sermon titles and brief descriptions below:

1. *Living the Interdependent Life.* This sermon is based on Hebrews 10:23–25, speaking of the interdependent relationship necessary for "stirring one another up." This message also speaks of the direction to which we cause one another to move: toward love and good works.

2. *Thinking Big in Small Things.* This sermon addresses the reality that Christian community is not an end for ourselves but instead a means for others. Stemming off of Hebrews 10:23–25, it walks through Acts 2, emphasizing the

attractiveness this type of community would have in a culture like ours.

3. *Jesus, Hope for the World.* This sermon walks through the unique focus the gospel of Luke brings to Jesus' ministry to the poor. If Jesus had a unique focus on the poor, then the question is: As his followers, do we?

February 2015: Bring on Ally full time to lead our relationship with the school district and to manage the relationship with Safe Families for Children. Bring on Dave to fill the pastoral role for the families/communities of Colossae who are engaging in this ministry. Teach the second two parts of the sermon series:

1. *Posture: Serving Others as Jesus Did.* This sermon piggybacks on the previous one by looking at three things Jesus did: (1) he gave himself, (2) he viewed generosity as a means of service, not power, and (3) he met people, not just needs.

2. *A Community Reaching Out.* This sermon paints the picture of this model and how it fits with the previous messages. It ends with a question-and-answer session with the whole congregation. Both Ally and Dave will be on the question and answer panel and will be available after each service.

March–May 2015: We will move forward in every aspect of this ministry. This includes but is not limited to: recruiting host families, encouraging communities, bridging the relationship between Safe Families for Children and the school district, implementing the processes of Safe Families and evaluating both quantitative and qualitative results.

Evaluation Process

Any ministry that requires resources should undergo evaluation. Our Safe Families for Children ministry was no different and was formally evaluated in June and December of 2015. The following served as general guidelines for what we evaluated:

1. The flow of communication between all parties
2. The quality of Colossae's relationship with civic leaders in district (did this deepen or weaken our relationship?)
3. The staffing roles, responsibilities, and follow-through
4. The number of families assisted
5. The number of children housed
6. The tensions and support structures to help in these areas
7. The number of first-time confessions of faith in Jesus

Table A

Primary Night Residence	Banks SD	Beaverton SD	Forest Grove SD	Gaston SD	Hillsboro SD	Sherwood SD	Tigard SD
Shelter, Transitional Housing		65	4		32	4	24
Doubled-Up Shared Housing	3	1092	66	1	247	38	84
Unsheltered (e.g., Car, Park, RV, Camping, Sub-standard Dwellings)		46	8		41	2	6
Motel or Hotel		62	4		34	3	11
Homeless, Unaccom-panied Youth Living in Unstable Housing		306	10		28	1	7

Table B

GRADE LEVEL	Banks SD	Beaverton SD	Forest Grove SD	Gaston SD	Hillsboro SD	Sherwood SD	Tigard SD
PRE-K		35	1			1	1
K		86	15		29	1	11
1	1	68	4		33	4	13
2	1	88	6		27	6	10
3		72	10		30	3	6
4		87	6		24	8	9
5		75	2		25	8	9
6		79	6		23	3	11

Table B (continued)

7		74	5		28	2	8
8		85	5		22	2	17
9		82	7		18	2	9
10		98	8		28	4	9
11	1	111	11	1	27	0	5
12		196	6		38	4	14
GED/ESD/OTHER	3	13	0	1	2	0	0
TOTAL # HOMELESS	3	1249	92	1	354	48	132
ENROLLMENT	1,230	39,494	5,976	520	20,955	5,158	12,363
% OF HOMELESS	.24%	3.16%	1.53%	.19%	1.68%	.93%	1.06%

COMPASSION CLINICS

OVERVIEW

A Compassion Clinic is a collaborative, free medical/ dental initiative led by the church body of your community to unite, serve, and transform for the gospel. This model of ministry started on the outskirts of Portland, Oregon, in 2006 and has seen incredible expansion through dozens of neighborhoods and cities. There is no one way or right way to run a clinic, as each community is unique and takes ownership of their clinic to create a context that is suited for their neighborhood's needs. Overall, we hope that each Compassion Clinic heals the broken with Jesus' love through the compassionate service of a united church.

A Compassion Clinic is:

- A united effort led by the local churches to unveil the love of God
- A catalytic movement that helps Christians serve together

- A free health and services event in the community for the underinsured
- An opportunity to draw together ministries, leaders, and organizations
- The beginning of ongoing relationships (both inside and outside the church)

THINGS TO CONSIDER

You may be motivated to begin a Compassion Clinic in your community for several reasons, but our hope is that no reason carries more weight than the desire to see the church reach the broken and hurting members of your community with the love of Jesus. Many motivations are birthed out of our compassion, our need to pursue justice, and more, but nothing will lead to a more successful Compassion Clinic than the desire to bring healing and hope to the hearts of your neighbors. Our hope is that your foundational desire of honoring God and reaching the lost and brokenhearted will lead to a healthy collaboration of local churches that plan and execute an amazing Compassion Clinic in your community.

We know how you feel as you face the realities of planning a large-scale free medical/dental outreach. It can seem intimidating and a long way off but, make no mistake, it is a vital opportunity for the church to make a bold statement in its community. As you begin the journey of details, meetings, and recruitment, don't forget that you are putting something together that has a much broader vision than pulling teeth or testing for high cholesterol. You are participating in a united effort of the church as a whole, and your acts of service will provide hundreds of others the opportunity to serve outside their comfort zone. When you step back and see the bigger picture, you see that all this effort leads to people being transformed by the gospel. It must be planned in a way that cultivates ongoing relationships with the community.

FIRST STEPS

Five to six months prior to possible clinic date you will need to:

- Gather a few interested leaders to discuss the possibilities
- Get a Compassion Clinic Toolkit (manuals, videos, etc.)
- Contact Compassion Connect
- Get two to three stake-holding churches together
- Consider one or two people who could lead a planning committee

For more information about hosting a Compassion Clinic in your neighborhood, please email serve@ compassionconnect.com or visit us online at www.com passionconnect.com.

GENERAL PLANNING COMMITTEE STRUCTURE

Most large Compassion Clinics provide both medical and dental services, and many may also offer vision, chiropractic, foot care, physical therapy, haircuts, a community resource fair, and even pet services. There is no limit to the services the church can choose to offer. The clinic leadership teams are divided up as follows:

- Medical
- Dental
- Connections
- Interpreters
- Shuttle service
- Financial team
- Food
- Hospitality
- Social services
- Equipment management
- Parking and safety

- Public relations
- Children's ministry
- Prayer team
- Appreciation team

Each team has its own leader who is represented on the steering committee as well as a group of general volunteers who assist on the day of the clinic. Equipment set up and volunteer orientation is done the night before the clinic.

BASIC FLOW

When guests arrive at the clinic, they fill out initial paperwork and self-select which services they would like to receive and then receive an appointment time. While guests wait for their appointments, they can pray with prayer team members, eat snacks or lunch provided by the food and hospitality teams, drop their children off at the children's area, or simply chat with anyone from the connections team who will make them feel loved and welcome. After their appointments, guests are welcome to stay and visit the social services fair or continue to visit with new friends and create a foundation that will hopefully lead to lasting relationships. After the clinic is over, the equipment team comes for cleanup and everyone can breathe a sigh of thankfulness about what God has done that day through the unity of his people!

As I have stated earlier in the book, this has been a simple means for building trust and a closer relationship with the school district. The needs of people are met in as an expression and belief in a good and loving God, but there is more to evaluate here. The goal is not to do a clinic. The clinic is a means to a much bigger end. If it is not helping building relationships—with people in need and the school district—shutting it down should be considered. If churches are not collaborating together after a few times, it should also be reevaluated. The power of serving in the schools is fully realized when people from all different churches are serving alongside one another. This larger kingdom picture is what we want to paint for our community. Someone has to start somewhere, so this type of collaboration might take a while to build. But if the building process stalls, continuing the event should be reevaluated.

Notes

1. Matthew 22:34–40.
2. See Appendix A for the full details of this program called "Safe Families."
3. In order to protect their privacy, some of the names in this chapter have been changed.
4. Katie Rose Quandt, "Poverty Is Rising Much Faster in Suburbs than in Cities," 25 January 2015, Moyers & Company, http://billmoyers.com/2015/01/29/suburban-poverty/.
5. Quoted in Quandt, "Poverty Is Rising."
6. Jennifer Swartvagher "Suburban Poverty, Hidden on Tree-Lined Streets," 13 January 2015, Motherlode, http://parenting.blogs.nytimes.com/2015/01/13/suburban-poverty-hidden-on-tree-lined-streets/?_r=0.
7. http://www.4uth.gov.ua/usa/english/society/rural/backgrnd/06rdiv/diverse.htm.
8. For details of how this is determined, see: http://www.census.gov/hhes/www/poverty/about/overview/measure.html.
9. http://www.ers.usda.gov/topics/rural-economy-population/rural-poverty-well-being/poverty-overview.aspx.
10. See Table A at the end of this Appendix, "Categories of Homeless Students per District for Washington County."
11. See Table B at end of Appendix A, "Disaggregated by Grade Level and School District Groups for Washington County for the 2013–2014 School Year."
12. David J. Bosch, *Believing in the Future: Toward a Missiology of Western Culture* (Harrisburg, Pa.: Trinity Press International, 1995), 59.
13. http://bethlambdin.net/2015/01/26/a-big-milestone-lets-do-this/.